# SUGAR CHANGED THE WORLD

# SUGAR CHANGED THE WORLD

### A Story of Magic, Spice, Slavery, Freedom, and Science

BY **MARC ARONSON** AND **MARINA BUDHOS**

HOUGHTON MIFFLIN HARCOURT

BOSTON • NEW YORK

For information about permission to reproduce selections from this book, write to trade.permissions@hmhco.com or to Permissions, Houghton Mifflin Harcourt Publishing Company, 3 Park Avenue, 19th Floor, New York, New York 10016.

www.hmhco.com

The text of this book is set in 14-point Adobe Jenson.

The Library of Congress has cataloged the hardcover edition as follows:
Aronson, Marc.
Sugar changed the world : a story of magic, spice, slavery, freedom, and science / by Marc Aronson and Marina Budhos.
p. cm.
Includes bibliographical references.
1. Sugar—History—Juvenile literature. 2. Sugar trade—History—Juvenile literature. 3. Slavery—History—Juvenile literature. 4. Liberty—History—Juvenile literature. 5. Passive resistance—History—Juvenile literature. I. Budhos, Marina Tamar. II. Title.
TP378.2.A767 2010
664'.109—dc22
2009033579

ISBN: 978-0-618-57492-6 hardcover
ISBN: 978-0-544-58247-7 paperback

Manufactured in China
SCP 16 15 14 13 12
4500821808

*To those who crossed seas to labor in sugar, and to
Dr. Sidney Mintz, who led the way in telling their stories.*

# CONTENTS

———

*Saccharum officinarum*, or sugar cane, as depicted in Robert Bentley and Henry Trimen's *Medicinal Plants* (1880 edition). (COURTESY HISTORY & SPECIAL COLLECTIONS FOR THE SCIENCES; LOUISE M. DARLING BIOMEDICAL LIBRARY, UCLA)

# PROLOGUE

## How We Came to Write This Book

———

## MARC

It was a typically hot, dry day in Jerusalem. Marina and I were sitting on a sun-warmed stone patio when I learned my family's sugar story. A cousin of mine was filling in a bit of our history that had always puzzled me.

My father's family came from Ukraine, then part of the Russian Empire, where his father, Solomon, the grand rabbi of Kiev, was the latest in a long line of rabbis that stretched back to the 1300s. Solomon was a forward-thinking rabbi who helped make bridges between the Jewish community and the Christians. He knew that change was coming, and he committed himself to building what was to become the land of Israel. My grandfather moved his family to Tel Aviv, where he became one of the leaders of the Jewish community.

One change he had not counted on, however, was his son Avram's choice of a wife. Avram, the eldest son, my uncle, was expected to become a rabbi—like the seventeen eldest sons before him. During World War I, though, when Avram was being held in a prisoner-of-war camp in Germany, he fell in love with a dusky-eyed Russian Christian. They married—against his father's fierce objections. Avram was exiled from his parents' home until his father was on his deathbed and forgave him.

Nina was always a mysterious figure in the family: beautiful as a movie star, cosmopolitan and elegant, with wide Slavic cheeks. She spoke only Russian, though she lived much of her adult life in Tel Aviv. There were rumors that she came from nobility and that she had once been very rich. She and Avram were thought of as a glamorous couple—he the charming man with his head in the clouds (in Yiddish the word for that kind of person is *luftmensh,* "air man"), she the mysterious beauty who had given up everything to be with him.

I wanted to know more about the beguiling Nina, and my cousin had plenty of stories to share. He told me that her grandfather was a Russian serf—a farmer who could be bought and sold by the noble who owned his land. Family legend has it that this serf, a remarkable and intelligent man, helped to change the course of the history of sugar. In the early 1800s, the British controlled most of the sugar plantations of the Caribbean and the sea routes to Europe. As a result, their rivals were desperate to find a new way to create sugar. They turned to beets.

We don't know exactly what Nina's grandfather's invention did, but as the story goes, he found a way to give raw beet sugar sparkling hues. People from Russia to the cafés of Vienna could now buy cheap and attractive sugar produced on European soil.

Serfs were much like slaves, since they had no choice about where they lived or worked. Yet Nina's grandfather made so much money from his invention that he was able to buy his freedom from his owner. He went on to become a very rich man—so rich, he not only bought a piece of land on the Volga River but married off his daughter to a noble who owned the next stretch of river lands. Together they could form a kind of mini empire, controlling a large swath of this important waterway, and they became the first family in the area to buy an automobile.

Unfortunately, the noble's son was very cruel, and Nina's mother eventually fled her marriage, went to the czar, and asked for an annulment. The czar explained that under the Russian Orthodox Church there were no divorces. However, if she gave him enough money, he would allow her and her daughter to leave Russia. So the daughter of the sugar inventor set off for Berlin with a young Nina, carrying diamonds and gold—almost all of which she lost during World War I.

All that was left of the fortune was one diamond, which Naomi, the daughter of Nina, kept tucked in a drawer in her home in Israel.

## MARINA

For me, the story of sugar began in a white house down in the Caribbean.

Ever since I was a little girl, I had heard about our house in Guyana. It was beautiful: a long white box with a series of windows, each shaded by delicate lattice shutters. Like all the houses in the area, where the land easily floods, it sat on slender stilts; underneath was what was called the bottomhouse, where the chickens strutted about. Inside was furniture imported from Poland, and gleaming wooden floors; stowed in the drawers were my aunts' gold and ruby and diamond jewelry, and their hand-sewn dresses, more intricate than the ordinary fare that the other village women wore.

My great-grandparents had come from India to Guyana—then

British Guiana—in the late nineteenth century to work on the sugar plantations. Sugar was the backbone of the British Empire at that time. The demand was huge, for sugar had gone from being a luxury that only kings could afford to a necessity. Even the poorest of London shopgirls took sugar in their tea.

Slavery was abolished in the British Empire in 1833, thirty years before the Emancipation Proclamation in the United States. But even after they freed their slaves, the sugar plantation owners were desperate to find cheap labor to cut cane and process sugar. So the British owners looked to another part of the empire—India—and recruited thousands of men and women, who were given five-year contracts and a passage back. For a person from India, going overseas was not a simple matter. Once you crossed the "black water" of the surrounding oceans, you were said to have "gone to tapu." You no longer had any place in your village and could not be accepted back until you went through a special ceremony. Leaving India truly meant giving up your home; yet for some—for my family—that was their only chance for a better life.

My family's white house was the dowry of my grandmother, a tall, light-skinned woman who came from a family that had prospered under the British plantation system. The house was built in Letter Kenny, a small village in the far eastern corner of Guyana, not far from the border with what is now Surinam. The family had some land and servants. My father used to talk about the canals where he would catch shrimp.

My great-grandfather had been chosen to be a *sirdar*, in charge of the field hands, and after his contract was over, he purchased land and prospered. That was how he was able to give away his daughter with a dowry of a large house to my grandfather, who also held good positions on several plantations. His decision to marry his children in the Christian

Church so that they all became converts meant they were seen as "above" the other villagers. They were a family that seemed to be moving up, especially the boys, who were bright and promising students. All the girls wore Western-style dresses, and the family ate imported luxuries such as marmalade and canned sardines. The boys were not expected to work in the fields. One daughter, Eileen, became a missionary, a bustling, sharp-eyed woman who sternly taught the local Sunday school. My father eventually won a scholarship in the United States, went to Howard University, which was recruiting students from the West Indies, and became a teacher.

Even when life got hard, when my father's older brothers had troubles, when my poor aunts were stranded in their senility and old age—taken care of by the villagers they'd once looked down upon—my family hung on to that house. They talked of the day when my brother and I would inherit the house, their proud symbol of one family's rise in a little British colony built on sugar.

Eventually, I visited Guyana to find out the fate of our house. As our car passed old sugar estates, and I saw the palm trees bending against the wide sky, the lush cane growing in thick, shiny rows, the villages, which were really parcels of land surrounding the important estates, I realized that sugar had been the entire reason for this country's existence. Every now and then an old boiling house—where the cane is processed into crystals, molasses, and rum—would show itself on the flat landscape, cropping up like a hulking ghost.

Once we got to Letter Kenny, we learned that our house was long gone, sold shortly before my aunts' deaths, a car repair shop in its place. All that was left were the last remnants of concrete and some old plumbing—and a history waiting to be told.

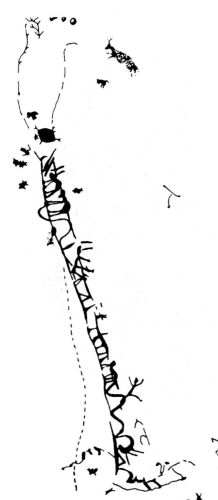

———————

The diamond and the house: two family treasures, two parts of the story of sugar. We realized that our two family stories—Marina's great-grandparents, brought to Guyana to replace slaves, and Marc's aunt's grandfather, helping to refine an alternative to that same sugar—were just the beginning of a much larger story about a remarkable substance. It is a story of the movement of millions of people, of fortunes made and lost, of brutality and delight—all because of tiny crystals stirred into our coffee, twirled on top of a cake. Sugar, we began to see, changed the world.

## THE AGE OF HONEY

There was a time before sugar, when those white grains that melt on your tongue did not exist anywhere on earth. Historians speak of the Iron Age, the Bronze Age—metals that were used in weapons and tools. But we could just as well speak of the first several thousand years of human history as the Age of Honey.

A rock drawing in Spain from about 7000 B.C. shows a man who has climbed a hillside, found a crevice holding a hive, and is reaching in to grab the honey. Indeed, a lucky wanderer in just about any part of Europe, Africa, or Asia that wasn't covered with ice could stumble on a hive and—at the risk of some stings—come away with a treat. (People in the Americas had no bees, so used syrups made from maple trees, agave cactus, or mashed fruits for their sweeteners.) Then someone figured out that you didn't have to be lucky. You could hollow out a log near bees, and they would make it their home. You could "keep" bees—you didn't have to find them.

These two rock drawings from Spain show bee hunters climbing cliffs to find honey. Made around 7000 B.C., they depict the earliest form of honey collecting. (EVA CRANE, WORLD HISTORY OF BEEKEEPING AND HONEY HUNTING)

In the Age of Honey, people tasted the neighborhood where they lived. From a light orange-blossom flavor that is almost a perfume to dark buckwheat with a hint of soil and grain, honey tastes like local flowers. And that was only part of its appeal. Bees work very hard, and it is easy to see that a queen bee is surrounded by worker bees that protect and serve her. To the ancients, a beehive was perfect, for it brought a gift of sweetness to people while being a mirror of their lives—a king or queen served by loyal subjects.

Honey was a way of living: People ate foods grown near them, did the same work as their parents and ancestors, and owed honor and respect to kings, nobles, those above them. Because bees in their hives seemed a model of how people should live, the Roman poet Virgil saw them as having a spark of the gods in them:

> *Some say that unto bees a share is given*
> *Of the Divine Intelligence*

Sugar is different from honey. It offers a stronger sweet flavor, and like steel or plastic, it had to be invented. In the Age of Sugar, Europeans bought a product made thousands of miles away that was less expensive than the honey from down the road. That was possible only because sugar set people in motion all across the world—millions of them as slaves, in chains; a few in search of their fortunes. A perfect taste made possible by the most brutal labor: That is the dark story of sugar. But there is another story as well. Information about sugar spread as human knowledge ex-

In this 1901 photograph, two boys enjoy eating cane, and very likely they also work in cane fields. The plant was both an energy source and a curse. (LIBRARY OF CONGRESS)

panded, as great civilizations and cultures exchanged ideas. In fact, while sugar was the direct cause of the expansion of slavery, the global connections that sugar brought about also fostered the most powerful ideas of human freedom.

Sugar is a taste we all want, a taste we all crave. People throughout the planet everywhere have been willing to do anything, anything at all, to get that touch of sweetness. We even know exactly how thrilling it was to taste sugar for the first time. When the Lewis and Clark Expedition met up with the Shoshone, who had little previous contact with Old World products, Sacagawea gave a tiny piece of sugar to a chief. He loved it, saying it was "the best thing he had ever tasted." Sugar created a hunger, a need, which swept from one corner of the world to another, bringing the most terrible misery and destruction, but then, too, the most inspiring ideas of liberty.

Sugar changed the world.

We begin that story with a man who could never know enough.

# PART ONE

# From Magic to Spice

The year is 326 B.C. Alexander the Great stands at the Indus River in what is now Pakistan. For a decade he and his Greek soldiers have been battling their way across the known world, defeating even the mighty Persians, rulers of Asia. Alexander's string of victories only feeds his hunger to conquer all, to know all. But his men balk. Tired of fighting, homesick, they refuse to go on. Alexander realizes he cannot continue to conquer Asia, but he is too curious to stop exploring. He has already built a fleet of eight hundred ships, appointed his close friend Nearchus captain, and sent them to investigate the coast of India by sea.

And it is Nearchus who stumbles upon the "sweet reed."

The Greeks knew something of India (actually the Indian subcontinent, the area that today includes the nations of India and Pakistan) from the books of Herodotus, a writer who lived about a century earlier. He reported that when the Persian emperor Darius I invaded India around 510 B.C., his men found a sweet reed that produced honey.

The reed the Persians found was probably sugar cane. The tall thin stalks of cane resemble bamboo: They have a woody bark marked off with knobs. Strip off the bark, and the grayish inside of the plant is moist and sweet—you can suck it between your teeth and drink in the juice. To this day you can find piles of sugar cane heaped in tropical markets—offering buyers a refreshing treat that is somewhere between a candy bar and an energy drink.

When Nearchus sailed off to explore, he too found the "reeds" that "produce honey, although there are no bees." The ever-curious Greeks were glad to learn of sugar cane, but it was just one more interesting fact about the natural world, the way a postcard from a summer vacation might list the sights a family has recently seen. No one could have imagined that those "reeds" would bring an end to the entire buzzing world of the Age of Honey.

## GODS AND RITUALS

Cane sugar can be traced back to the island now called New Guinea, which is just north of Australia. Cane was probably first cultivated by humans on the island some five thousand years or more before the Greeks. At first, cane was simply a wild plant that tasted good. Then people figured out how to grow it, just as they learned how to plant apple trees or berry bushes. From New Guinea, knowledge of the sweet plant slowly spread north to the Asian mainland. Polynesian seafarers also took canes with them as they sailed from island to island until they reached Hawaii around A.D. 1100.

But it is in India, where it was used as an offering in religious and magical ceremonies, that we have the first written record of sugar.

Long before the first pyramids were built in Egypt, the ancient Sumerians traded with the people of Harappa and Mohenjo Daro, who lived along the Indus River. Unfortunately, we are still not able to read the writings left behind from those ancient cities. So the first documents telling us about life in that region come from a much later period. These

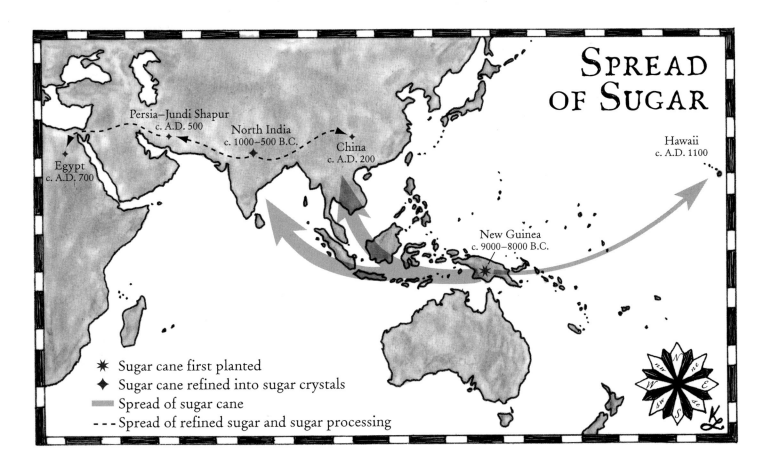

Preparing an image of Durga for a festival in her honor. This photograph was taken recently in India, where she is actively worshiped today. (COURTESY RAM RAHMAN)

This diagram from the *Atharva Veda* shows how to place a triangular fire pot to make an offering to Durga. The signs surrounding the triangle indicate that the altar should have one angle facing south. (REPRODUCED FROM AN 1889 EDITION OF THE AMERICAN JOURNAL OF PHILOLOGY)

Hindu sacred teachings were probably first gathered together sometime between 1500 and 900 B.C., and were carefully memorized. Only hundreds of years later were they finally written down. The Hindu writings tell us of a religion in which fire was extremely important. People believed that the gods gave fire to human beings. Yet fire was also a way for humans to reach the gods. By placing offerings in a special fire, a priest could turn them into smoke and send them on to the gods. Five ingredients were selected for this special burning: milk, cheese, butter, honey, and sugar cane.

One of these early Hindu writings, the *Atharva Veda*, speaks of an archer's bow made of sugar cane. It tells of growing a circle of sugar cane as a kind of sweet protection for a lover, and it includes specific instructions on how to use sugar cane. To worship and request help from Durga, the most important goddess, you lie down and face a three-cornered fire pot. Then, as you speak the sacred words, you place your offerings in the fire.

Sugar cane was now an ingredient in ceremonies involving fire. Maybe after many, many offerings a priest noticed that if the juice of the cane was boiled in the right way, it crystallized into sweet, dark brown clumps. Perhaps that transformation itself seemed magical—a heated liquid turning into something that looked like dark grains of sand. In the *Atharva Veda*, sugar cane is called *ikshu*, which means "something that people want, or desire, because of its sweetness." But once people learned how to make sugar crystals, they began to use the name *sharkara*, which also meant "gravel."

Though Indians used sugar in rituals, they also enjoyed eating chunks of sugar cane. The word for "a piece of sugar" in the ancient Indian language of Sanskrit is *khanda*, which, as it passed through Persian to Arabic to Europe, became *candy*. Sugar had a third use in ancient India—it was considered a medicine. Today we say, "a spoonful of sugar helps the medicine go down." But from ancient times until quite recently, sugar itself was a medicine, a means of healing.

The next step in the spread of sugar came through a university that was the crossroads of all the world's knowledge.

## The World's First True University

Today, few people have heard of Jundi Shapur. But in its time, it was an exceptional university. Jundi Shapur was built in what is now Iran some-

Sugar continued to be planted in India in modern times. This drawing was made in 1854. Whether elephants actually pulled plows this way or a visiting artist just imagined that is unclear. (LIBRARY OF CONGRESS)

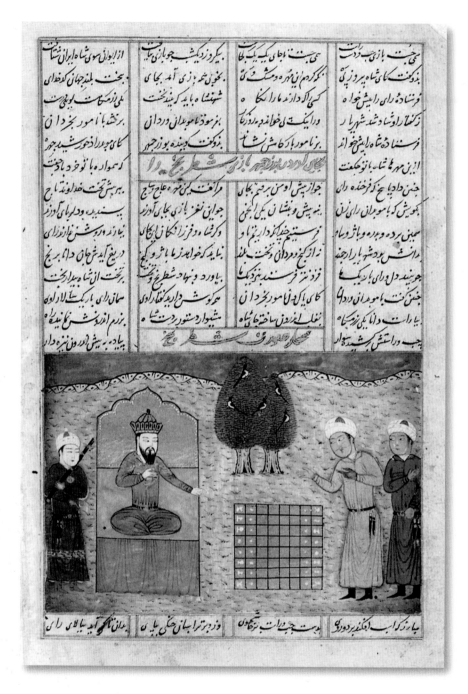

Kasra Anushirvan (Kasra the Just) was the ruler of the Sassanid empire from 531 to 579, when the academy of Jundi Shapur was the world center of knowledge. Here he receives an ambassador from India, who is showing him the game of chess. Apparently chess was introduced to Persia during his reign—and it is exactly that kind of exchange of ideas and knowledge that took place at Jundi Shapur. This image is an illustration from the Persian epic poem *The Shahnama*, which begins in the mythic past but includes a sequence of real rulers. Firdawsi's poem has been illustrated many ways, and you can see more than six thousand of those images by going to the website of the Shahnama Project (see the Web Guide to Color Images on page 131). This drawing is from a 1437 edition made in India. ("CHESS SENT TO ANUSHIRVAN" OR, 1403, F419V, BRITISH LIBRARY)

time between the 400s and mid-500s A.D. We can only guess the dates, but we do know more about the school. It was the meeting place of the world's great minds. In 529, Christians closed the school of Athens—the last link to the academies of Socrates, Plato, and Aristotle. The remaining Greek scholars moved to Jundi Shapur. Jews joined them, as did a group of Christians called Nestorians, who had their own ancient and scholarly traditions. Persians added their voices, and one of their learned doctors set off for what is now India, to gather and translate the wisdom of the Hindus. The school created the very first teaching hospital in the world, a place where the sick were treated and young doctors learned their craft, as well as a fine ob-servatory to track the heavens. At Jundi Sha-pur the best scholars west of China all gathered to think and study together.

By the 600s, the doctors at the school were writing about a medicine from India named *sharkara* or, as the Persians called it, *shaker*—sugar. Indeed, scholars at Jundi Shapur in-vented new and better ways to refine cane into sugar. Since the school had links with many of the great civilizations of Asia, the Mediterranean, and Europe, word of sugar and the experience of tasting its special sweetness began to spread. But that does not mean people were baking sweet cakes and topping them with sugary icing.

Today we generally think of sweet things as completely different from salty ones; we

Kasra is honored to this day: This statue of him graces the walls of the judicial palace in Iran's capital city of Tehran. (COURTESY KDI, IRAN)

eat fruit for breakfast, and if we eat meat as a main course, it is usually at lunch or dinner. But in those days, if people used fruit, honey, and sugar to sweeten foods, they often mixed salty or even bitter tastes with sweet ones. We still sometimes do that today: For example, gingerbread mixes sugar with spices such as ginger, clove, and nutmeg. A salty ham may have a sweet glaze; a Thanksgiving plate will often have both turkey and cranberry sauce. Foods such as these, which are eaten on holidays, often preserve tastes and ways of cooking from earlier times.

When knowledge of sugar was just beginning to spread from India, from Persia, from Greece, from the great school of Jundi Shapur, cooks working for the wealthiest people treated it as a spice, blending it with other tastes. They continued to do that for another thousand years. But the world of sugar was about to grow very rapidly—spread by a storm unlike any the world had ever seen: Islam.

## The Storm of God

When the prophet Muhammad began preaching in A.D. 610, he attracted only a few disciples. Yet by the time he died in 632, his faith had spread throughout Arabia. By 642, the armies of Muslim conquerors, along with the arguments of the Muslim faithful, took the religion all across Syria, Iraq, parts of Iran, and Egypt. From there, Islam spread through North Africa along the Mediterranean, across to the Iberian Peninsula, and over to France. Islam's march into Europe ended in 732, when the French defeated the Muslim armies at the battle of Poitiers. But that was not all. Muslim rulers took Alexander's old lands in Afghanistan and then, from there, swept through to conquer northern

India. The pagan tribes of Central Asia chose Islam. By conversion or conquest, Islam, the religion of Muhammad, won over nearly all the lands of the ancient world: Egypt, Persia, India, and the Christian Mediterranean.

The vast Muslim world was wonderful for the growth of knowledge. The Greeks had developed a level of practical experience and technical understanding a thousand years more advanced than anyone else nearby. The Muslims began to translate some of these ancient Greek texts. From India, Muslims learned of the zero, which allowed them to invent what we still call "Arabic" numerals. And because the Koran, the sacred book of Islam, is written in Arabic, scholars throughout the Muslim world learned to read Arabic and to share their knowledge. The Muslims swept past Jundi Shapur and learned the secrets of sugar. As they conquered lands around the Mediterranean Sea, they spread word of how to grow, mill, and refine the sweet reed.

Masters of sugar, the Muslims began to use it in lavish displays. Combining sugar with almonds—as is still done in marzipan—cooks who were serving wealthy Muslims built elaborate, edible sculptures. One Muslim ruler filled a feast table with seven large palaces made of sugar; another displayed an entire tree made of sugar. Sugar was now a Muslim luxury, a sign of the wealth and generosity of Islamic emperors and kings.

With the rise of Islam, Egypt became the world's great sugar laboratory. The kind of sugar easiest to produce from cane is dark—the color comes from molasses, which also makes that form of sugar spicy and even bitter. What we call molasses is just a natural part of the first grinding of sugar cane into syrup. Sugar refiners drain out the dark molasses to use by itself and are left with relatively white sugar. The noble and wealthy, who could afford sugar, wanted it to be as pure, sweet, and white as possible. The Egyptians figured out how to meet that need.

After the Egyptians crushed cut cane and captured the juice, they boiled and strained the liquid, let it settle, then strained it again. The cane juice was now poured into molds with holes in the bottom, so that all the liquid could drain out, leaving only a powder. That powder was then mixed with milk and boiled again. After one round of these steps, the process was repeated all over again. As a result of all this effort and care, Egypt was known for the "whitest and purest" sugar.

The world of sugar centered on the Muslim Mediterranean, but it also stretched as far as China to the east and even Europe to the north. Marco Polo visited the empire of Kublai Khan in the 1280s. He noted that while the Chinese had known how to grow cane and produce brown sugar for over a thousand years, it was "certain Egyptians at the Khan's court" who explained how to make the dazzling white sugar coveted by so many.

While the Islamic world was spreading and absorbing new knowledge, enjoying the taste of sugar, Europe had gone the opposite way: isolation.

This 1501 print shows two kinds of computation. The person on the right side is the ancient Greek philosopher Pythagoras (who lived in the mid-500s B.C.). He is using objects to count. The person on the left is Boethius, a Christian from about a thousand years later, who is using Arabic numerals. Between them is the spirit, or muse, of arithmetic. In fact, Europeans did not begin to learn about Arabic numbers until much closer to the time this drawing was made, around A.D. 1200. (LIBRARY OF CONGRESS)

## FORTRESS EUROPE

Picture a feast in a medieval castle. You'll have to guess, because there were no cookbooks in Christian Europe until the 1100s. And why should there have been? Cooks had no reason to be able to read or write. Wealthy lords could afford meat. Poor people ate bread. When a lord had a feast, he served meat on

ATLANTIC OCEAN

France

Italy

Spain

Sicily

BLACK SEA

MEDITERRANEAN SEA

Crete

Cyprus

Syria

Egypt

AREAS WHERE SUGAR CANE WAS GROWN

AFTER A.D. 700 NEAR THE MEDITERRANEAN

bread—instead of using plates, people ate on "trenchers," which were just slabs of stale bread.

Ever since A.D. 400, when invaders rampaged through Rome and the Roman Empire began to crumble, Europe had become increasingly violent, ignorant, and divided. While Muslims studied the words of the ancient Greeks, most Europeans turned to counting on their hands, and only a few knew how to read. Except for some merchants looking for business, no one ventured very far. The outside world was just that—a long distance away. Still, from what we can tell, everyone, rich or poor, liked to flavor their food with spices—a taste that may well date back to Roman times.

Even though one book after another repeats this myth, the popu-

The Ottomans, the Muslim rulers of an empire based in what is now Turkey, were masters of sugar sculpture. In 1720, when the Turkish painter Levni depicted the celebration for the circumcision of Sultan Ahmed III's son, his huge sculptures of gardens were made entirely out of sugar; the pieces were so heavy, it took eighteen men to carry each one. This is a picture of one of them. (COURTESY TOPKAPI PALACE MUSEUM AND DR. NURHAN ATASOY)

larity of spices had nothing to do with disguising the taste of meat or fish that had gone bad. Any lord who could afford spices (which were expensive) could easily get fresh meat or fish (which were readily available); and when a cook happened to be stuck with rancid food, the spices he had available could not hide the awful smell or taste. Whenever they could, people used the spices that were so popular, they became an expensive necessity: pepper, ginger, sugar, sometimes saffron. Only the very rich could afford the luxuries—such as ambergris (which is coughed up by whales and offers a strange, perfumy taste of the sea).

In the 1100s, the richest Europeans slowly began to add more flavor to their food—because of a series of fairs and wars. A smart count in the Champagne region of France guaranteed the safety of any merchant coming to sell or trade at the markets in the lord's lands. Soon word spread, and the fairs flourished. Starting around 1150, the six Champagne fairs became the one place where Europeans could buy and sell products from the surrounding world—a first step in connecting them to the riches and tastes beyond. Fortress Europe was slowly opening up.

## THE CHAMPAGNE FAIRS

The markets began in January, in Lagny-sur-Marne, near Paris. For two months, merchants from cold northern Europe came to trade with businessmen from warm Italy. One after another, five more French cities held fairs, until the last one of the year ended in Troyes in December, and then the cycle started again.

The fairs were very well organized. They featured covered galleries so that merchants could buy and sell even if rain came drumming down; cellars were so large, they resembled underground cities. At the fairs, merchants could trust the weights and measures, and a strict order prevailed for how things were to be sold. For the first twelve days one could sell only woven cloth—which is what the traders from northern Europe brought. Then the "sergeants" of the fair would walk through the streets crying, "Pack up, pack up," and all the cloth must be put away. Now the leather traders, who came from as far as Spain, and the fur merchants, whose goods might come from Russia, filled the tables with piles of hides and pelts.

In 1420 a master chef in what is now Italy wrote that a wild boar's head such as this needed to be green on one side—glazed with a sauce made of parsley—and covered with gold foil on the other. Medieval nobles wanted their food to be a lavish display of color, special effects (such as making one kind of food appear to be another), and scent. Spices were expensive and came from the mysterious east, which made them a necessary part of any nobleman's banquet. Sugar was considered a spice, though not the rarest and most expensive. This photo is from a modern book that faithfully reproduces medieval recipes. (COURTESY CLAUDE HUYGHENS)

The traders who came up from Italy offered items they had bought from Muslims, which were not available in Europe: fruits such as oranges, apricots, and figs; dyes such as cochineal, which produces a rich red; rare fabrics such as cotton and raw silk. Many of the fabrics that we know of today came to Europe via the Muslims, and their names still show their origins: damask from Damascus, muslin from Mosul, gauzes from Gaza.

The Italian merchants sometimes sailed across the Mediterranean Sea to Syria, where they could buy black pepper that had been grown on the southwest coast of India. The tiny dried black peppercorns were the perfect item to trade, because the small ships of the time could carry enough to make a nice profit. From India the pepper was shipped across to Arabia, where camel caravans would carry it all the way to Syria. The Italians could purchase enough pepper in Syria to carry with them to the next Champagne fair. Every count whose cook added the bite of costly black pepper to his food knew he was getting a taste of far distant lands. As late as 1300, Jean de Joieville, a French writer who had actually lived in the Muslim world, still believed that these spices came from the outer edges of the Garden of Eden, located somewhere along the river Nile. There, people "cast their nets outspread into the river, at night; and when morning comes, they find in their nets such goods as . . . ginger, rhubarb, wood of aloes, and cinnamon."

Next to the mounds of fruits and spices at the fairs were piles of a medicine that the Italians also bought from the Muslims: sugar. "Nice white sugar . . . when taken moderately cleans the blood, strengthens body and mind, especially chest, lungs and throat," noted a physician in the 1500s. He did, though, point out that it "makes the teeth blunt and makes them decay."

Since sugar had to pass through many hands before it reached the fairs, it was expensive and hard to get. King Henry III of England, for example, liked sugar. Yet there was little he could do to satisfy his craving. He wrote to one official in 1226 asking if he could possibly obtain three pounds of the precious substance—at a cost of about 450 modern dollars. He later appealed to a mayor, hoping he might be able to get four more pounds of the rare grains. And finally, by 1243, he managed to buy three hundred pounds.

The fairs lasted until the 1300s, when Venice came to dominate European trade with the Muslim world. The Venetians greatly expanded the sugar trade, so much so that a hundred years after Henry III's reign, the English were able to buy thousands of pounds of the sweet stuff each year. Perhaps their taste for it grew because Europeans had been exposed to sugar in a different way: through war.

## OUT OF WAR COMES SWEETNESS

According to the Gospels, Jesus lived and died in what is now Israel. Christianity was born there and in cities near the Mediterranean. But with the rise and spread of Islam, those holy lands were no longer ruled by Christians. In 1095 Pope Urban II rallied the Christians of western Europe to set out on a great mission to take back those sacred lands. We know these wars as the Crusades—bloody, gruesome conflicts, the scars of which are felt in the Middle East to this day. But the Crusades were more than battles; they were also an information exchange. As a result of their contact with Muslims, the Europeans began to break out of their sealed-off world. They learned mathematics and, according to some scholars, how to build windmills. Windmills were a great power

Painted around 1490 by the French artist Robinet Testard, this picture shows people collecting aloe wood as it floats down a river from the Garden of Eden. Aloe grows in Southeast and East Asia, so the Europeans knew little about it. They were willing to believe that aloe, like ginger and cinnamon, could be found only by gathering twigs that drifted away from paradise. Much like incense today, spices were thought of as having almost mystical, spiritual qualities. (NATIONAL LIBRARY OF RUSSIA, ST. PETERSBURG, MS FR. V. VI., FOL. 143)

source that allowed Europeans to drain swamps and make use of lands that had previously gone to waste. With more land, they could grow more food. This knowledge that Muslims had helped Europe to get on its feet. And wars against the Muslims brought Europeans to sugar.

As they marched to the Holy Land, Christians noticed "certain ripe plants which the common folk called 'honey cane' and which were much like reeds. . . . In our hunger we chewed them all day because of the taste of honey."

The Christian Crusades in the Holy Lands failed, as the Europeans could not hold on to any sites taken from the Muslims for very long. But Christians did control fertile islands in the Mediterranean, such as Sicily, Cyprus, and Rhodes. There they began to apply skills they had learned from the Muslims: how to plant sugar cane, and how to refine sugar. That was valuable knowledge, because while it is not hard to grow sugar cane, farmers who plan on making sugar itself face a special challenge.

## The Problem with Sugar Cane

There are two problems with cane if you want to make vast amounts of sugar: one of time and the other of fire. Growers claimed that the instant a knife sliced the stalks, the sweet mass inside started to harden and turn woody. Apparently, if they did not get the cane into the boiling vat within forty-eight hours—preferably twenty-four hours—their crop would be ruined. Whether or not that speed was absolutely necessary, owners insisted on it. They may also have been thinking of pure economics: Once you cut cane, it begins to dry out. Piles of cane are heavy, bulky, and hard to move, while sugar in tiny crystals can be packed into barrels and shipped by water. Cane loses money as long as it sits, and is on its way to making money once it has been made into sugar. For the growers, time truly was money.

The only way to make a lot of sugar is to engineer a system in which an army of workers swarms through the fields, cuts the cane, and hauls the pile to be crushed into a syrup that flows into the boiling room. There, laboring around the clock, workers cook and clean the bubbling liquid so that the sweetest syrup turns into the sweetest sugar. This is not farming the way men and women had done it for thousands of years in the Age of Honey. It is much more like a factory, where masses of people must do every step right, on time, together, or the whole system collapses.

The Muslims worked out a new form of farming to handle sugar, which came to be called the sugar plantation. A plantation was not a new technology but, rather, a new way of organizing planting, growing, cutting, and refining a crop. On a regular farm there may be cows, pigs, and chickens; fields of grain; orchards filled with fruit—many different kinds of foods to eat or sell. By contrast, the plantation had only one purpose: to create a single product that could be grown, ground, boiled, dried, and sold to distant markets. Since one cannot live on sugar, the crop grown on plantations could not even feed the people who harvested it. Never before in human history had farms been run this way, as machines designed to satisfy just one craving of buyers who could be thousands of miles away.

On a plantation there were large groups of workers—between fifty and several hundred. The mill was right next to the crop, so that growing and grinding took place in the same spot. And all the work was governed by extremely tight, rigid discipline. The Muslims began to put together the rules for this new kind of farming. Both they and the Christians experimented with using their slaves to run the plantations.

This drawing made around 1623 shows slaves doing all of the tasks involved in creating sugar: Under the hot sun, they harvest the crop (top right); the cut stalks are gathered into bundles (front right) and carried to the mill (right); the cane is ground under a turning wheel (left center), then poured into vats to be boiled (left front); sugar crystals are then ladled into jars to cool (left center). No real mill would have looked exactly like this. The picture was meant to show the whole sugar cycle at a glance. (LIBRARY OF CONGRESS)

At first many of the slaves working sugar plantations in the Mediterranean were Russians, or anyone captured in war. But even all this careful organization did not solve the second problem with sugar.

In order to keep those vats boiling, a great deal of wood to burn was needed. (Later on, sugar planters figured out that they could use the crushed cane stalks as fuel.) Not many places in the world offer rich lands that can grow cane, are near water so that the sugar can be easily shipped to distant shores, and are filled with trees ready to be cut down. The sugar plantation solved the management problem of cutting and refining a large crop, but it did not supply growers with the forests they would need to cut down in order to boil the sugar syrup.

In the 1400s, Spain and Portugal were competing to explore down the coast of Africa and find a sea route to Asia. That way, they could have the prized Asian spices they wanted without having to pay high prices to Venetian and Muslim middlemen. Spanish and Portuguese sailors searching for that sea route conquered the Canary Islands and the Azores. Soon they began building Muslim-style sugar plantations on the islands, some of them staffed by slaves purchased from nearby Africa. One sailor came to know these islands particularly well because he traded in "white gold"—sugar. And then, as he set off on his second voyage across the sea to what he thought was Asia, he carried sugar cane plants from Gomera, one of the Canary Islands, with him on his ship.

His name was Christopher Columbus.

# PART TWO

# Hell

Welcome to Hell.

It is early morning on a Caribbean island, and African slaves—hundreds of them—are being sent out to the fields to pull weeds and burn the high, dry grass. Bent over, palms callused from the small, tough stalks, smoke scorching their eyes, they work. The overseer prowls nearby, mounted on horseback, a rawhide whip fastened to his saddle.

The plants that Columbus brought with him to the island he called Hispaniola (now Haiti and the Dominican Republic) flourished. Soon there were sugar plantations all over the island, and a kind of "white gold" rush began. More and more

Europeans saw growing sugar in the New World with slave labor as the road to vast wealth. Sugar planting boomed first on Hispaniola. When news spread of the gold of the Aztecs in nearby Mexico, farming could not hold the interest of Spaniards. But that only gave other Europeans the opportunity to take the lead in seeking sugar fortunes.

The Europeans next made Brazil the center of sugar (with the Catholic Portuguese and the Protestant Dutch battling for control). The British followed by turning Barbados into a sugar island; then the French found rich soil on Hispaniola all over again. The more sugar was planted, the more mills were built to grind it, the more docks were hammered into place to ship sugar, the more enslaved people were brought from Africa to work the plantations.

The first European boat reached Brazil in 1500—it was an accident. Pedro Cabral was trying to sail around Africa to Asia to buy spices for his native Portugal, and the ocean current took him to Brazil instead. That same strong current made it easy to bring slaves across the Atlantic to Brazil, and over the next four hundred years some three million Africans were taken to Brazil. As the common saying went: "Without sugar, no Brazil; without slaves, no sugar; without Angola, no slaves."

In just over one hundred years, between 1701 and 1810, 252,500 enslaved Africans were brought to Barbados—an island that occupies only 166 square miles (making it, today, one of the smallest countries in the world). The English then set out to conquer more sugar islands, starting with Jamaica, which they took from Spain in 1665. In the same period that the 252,500 Africans were brought to Barbados, 662,400 Africans were taken to Jamaica. Thus, sugar drove more than 900,000 people into slavery, across the Atlantic, to Barbados and Jamaica—and these were just two of the sugar islands. The English

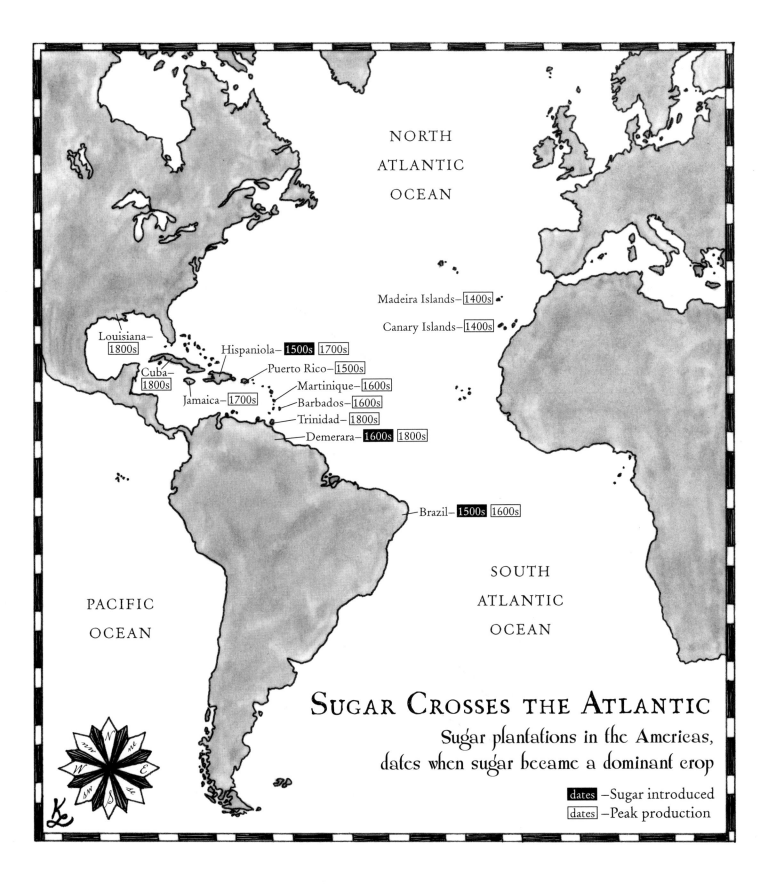

Madeira Islands— 1400s

Canary Islands— 1400s

Louisiana— 1800s

Hispaniola— **1500s** 1700s

Cuba— 1800s

Puerto Rico— 1500s

Jamaica— 1700s

Martinique— 1600s

Barbados— 1600s

Trinidad— 1800s

Demerara— **1600s** 1800s

Brazil— **1500s** 1600s

NORTH ATLANTIC OCEAN

SOUTH ATLANTIC OCEAN

PACIFIC OCEAN

## Sugar Crosses the Atlantic

Sugar plantations in the Americas,
dates when sugar became a dominant crop

**dates** —Sugar introduced

dates —Peak production

were eagerly filling Antigua, Nevis, Saint Kitts, and Montserrat with slaves and sugar mills. They took over much of Dutch Guiana for the same reason.

Seeing the fortunes being made in sugar, the French started their own scramble to turn the half of the island of Hispaniola that they

The best sugar land in Brazil was in the northeast coastal region called Pernambuco. This map from the 1600s shows boats coming to and fro, as well as the kind of sugar mill that was run by enslaved Africans. By 1640, when Pernambuco was briefly ruled by the Dutch, its plantations sent some twenty-four thousand pounds of sugar to Amsterdam alone. When the Portuguese regained control of the area, the Dutch fled to the Caribbean, bringing knowledge of how to grow sugar with them. Some Dutch Jews also escaped to New York, establishing the first Jewish community in the city. And as the Dutch and Portuguese battled to control Pernambuco, many Africans escaped and created a kingdom of their own called Palmares. (LIBRARY OF CONGRESS)

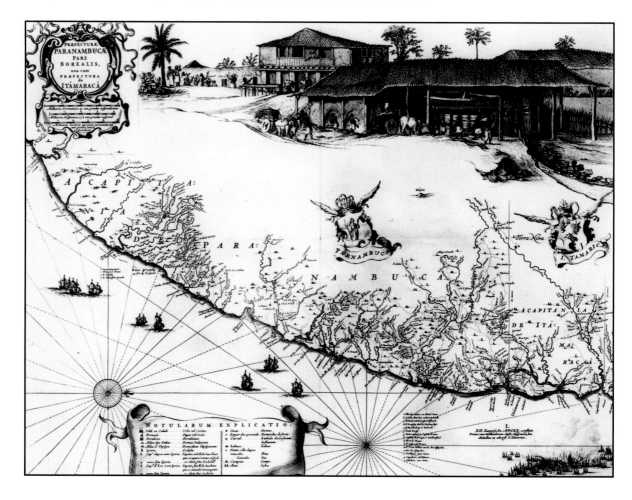

controlled (which is now Haiti), as well as Martinique, Guadeloupe, and French Guiana (along the South American coast near Dutch Guiana), into their own sugar colonies, which were filled with hundreds of thousands more African slaves. By 1753, British ships were taking an average of 34,250 slaves from Africa every year, and by 1768, that number had reached 53,100.

The sugar that piled up on the docks near the plantations was something new in the world: pure sweetness, pure pleasure, so cheap that common people could afford it. Scientists have shown that people all over the world must learn to like salty tastes, sour tastes, mixed tastes. But from the moment we are born, we crave sweetness. Cane sugar was the first product in human history that perfectly satisfied that desire. And the bitter lives of the enslaved Africans produced so much sugar that pure sweetness began to spread around the world.

Between the 1600s and the 1800s, sugar drove the entire economy linking Europe, Africa, Asia, and the Americas. The true Age of Sugar had begun—and it was doing more to reshape the world than any ruler, empire, or war had ever done.

## A Cycle of Death and Sweetness

The millions of Africans taken to work in sugar were not taught to read and write. They were not meant to speak, but to work. Olaudah Equiano, who lived from approximately 1745 to 1797, later claimed that he was an African taken to Barbados to work in sugar. He did learn to write, and recounted his life story in an autobiography. Equiano described what it was like to arrive in Barbados and to be sold off to the sugar planters:

*We were conducted immediately to the merchant's yard, where we were all pent up together, like so many sheep in a fold. . . . On a signal given (as the beat of a drum), the buyers rush at once into the yard where the slaves are confined, and make choice of that parcel that they like best.*

Because he was slight and sickly (as well as smart and useful), Equiano managed not to be sold to a plantation. So while his words take us from Africa to the sugar islands, even his memoir does not take us to the fields. That means we cannot hear the voices of the Africans directly. To tell their story, we must begin with what they did—how sugar shaped their lives.

For an African, whether you were sent to the Caribbean or South America, you were now part of the sugar machine. And it did not much matter where your ship landed. You could be working the fertile fields of Brazil or the hills of Jamaica; the brutal cycle of making sugar was much the same.

If the terrain was not too rocky or hilly, you might be part of a group of slaves who drove teams of oxen to draw plows across the fields. On rougher ground, you were sent out to clear a space five inches deep and five feet square. Then you dug holes for the cane shoots in the cleared squares. You needed to work quickly and without stopping. Overseers watched closely to make sure of that, beating slaves who did not carve out at least twenty-eight holes an hour on one French island. The painstaking work had just one aim: to plant a crop that would end up taking the life of every worker who touched it. As Equiano explained, the sugar slaves could hardly rest even when their day was done.

# The Spherical Trade

If you walked down Beekman Street in New York in the 1750s, you would come to a general store owned by Gerard Beekman—his family gave the street its name. The products on his shelves showed many of the ways sugar was linking the world. Beekman and merchants like him shipped flour, bread, corn, salted beef, and wood to the Caribbean. They brought back sugar, rum, molasses, limes, cocoa, and ginger. Simple enough; but this trade up and down the Atlantic coast was part of a much larger world system.

Textbooks talk about the Triangle Trade: Ships set out from Europe carrying fabrics, clothes, and simple manufactured goods to Africa, where they sold their cargoes and bought people. The enslaved people were shipped across the Atlantic to the islands, where they were sold for sugar. Then the ships brought sugar to North America, to be sold or turned into rum—which the captains brought back to Europe. But that neat triangle—already more of a rectangle— is completely misleading.

Beekman's trade, for example, could cut out Europe entirely. British colonists' ships set out directly from New York and New England carrying the food and timber that the islands needed, trading them for sugar, which the merchants brought back up the coast. Then the colonists traded their sugar for English fabrics, clothes, and simple manufactured goods, or they took their rum directly to Africa to buy slaves—to sell to the sugar islands. English, North American, French, and Dutch ships competed to supply the Caribbean plantations and buy their sugar. And even all these boats filling the waters of the Atlantic were but one part of an even larger system of world trade.

Africans who sold other Africans as slaves insisted on being paid in fabrics from India. Indeed, historians have discovered that some 35 percent of the cargo typically taken from Europe to Africa originally came from India. What could the Europeans use to buy Indian cloth? The Spanish shipped silver from the mines of Bolivia to Manila in the Philippines, and bought Asian products there. Any silver that English or French pirates could steal from the Spanish was also ideal for buying Asian cloth. So to get the fabrics that would buy the slaves that could be sold for sugar for the English to put into their tea, the Spanish shipped silver to the Philippines, and the French, English, and Dutch sailed east to India. What we call a triangle was really as round as the globe.

*Their huts, which ought to be well covered, and the place dry where they take their little repose, are often open sheds, built in damp places; so that when the poor creatures return tired from the toils of the field, they contract many disorders, from being exposed to the damp air in this uncomfortable state.*

Next came the seeders, whose job was to push cane cuttings into the cane holes or the rows made by the plows, and cover them with soil. If the cane took root and began to send off shoots, the weeding gang followed.

As a weeder, your job was to carefully pick away the undergrowth that could choke the cane stalks and stop them from growing tall enough, or that might attract vermin. Cleaning and weeding was done as many as three times while the cane grew, and it was some of the worst labor. A weeder spent ten to fourteen hours a day bent over with a hoe, digging out the unwanted growths at the base of the knobby cane stalks, ignoring the rats that might scuttle over his or her feet or the bladelike leaves that slashed at the worker's wrists and arms. Rats were everywhere—the records from one plantation in Jamaica report three thousand of them captured in just six months.

Because it did not require great arm strength, weeding was often done by women, young boys, or slight men. On the islands, this group of workers was called "the hogmeat gang." Sometimes, though, the weeding was done in a more thorough and dangerous way—with fire. The tangle of unwanted plants was set alight, but fire is not easy to control, and there was always the chance that high winds—or the anger of brutalized slaves—might whip up the flames, and soon a roaring blaze would engulf the fields.

You might be lucky enough to be trained as a specialist—the person who watched the cane grow and who kept an eye out for when the plants were ripe and ready to be cut. Special knowledge did not make a slave any less a slave—you were neither freed or paid. But perhaps some of the enslaved people had the personal pleasure of realizing that they had knowledge that the plantation owners needed. And if the best workers got even a little more to eat, a few moments more rest, they had a chance to be among the few who lived long enough to have children and to see them grow up.

While the plants ripened, one large group of slaves was sent off to cut the wood to fire the boiling vats, while another spent its days carting the timber back to the boiling house. This hard work led up to the all-important harvest.

In Brazil, when word came that the harvest was about to begin, a priest came to bless the mill—and the workers. The blessing was like the whistle at the start of a race, for now everything sped up. Slaves were given long, sharp machetes, which would be their equipment—but for some also their weapons—until the harvest was done. The cutters worked brutal, seemingly endless shifts during the harvest—for the hungry mills crushed cane from four in the afternoon to ten the next morning, stopping only in the midday heat. Slaves had to make sure there was just enough cane to feed the turning wheels during every one of those eighteen hours. They worked in teams, a man slashing the cane, a woman binding every twelve stalks into a bundle. According to one report from 1689, each pair of workers was expected to cut and bind 4,200 stalks a day. Exactly how much they cut depended on how much their mill could handle—the cutting must never get a day ahead of the grinding, for then the sugar cane would dry up.

Cutting cane was hard work, but it was nothing like what came next: Piles of freshly cut cane had to be fed into the ever-turning mill wheels, until they were completely crushed. The owners insisted that during the work hours the grinding never stop, no matter what. The mills were most often tended by women who were doing dangerous work while getting almost no rest. That was a very bad combination. An ax was often propped up near the rollers so if a slave closed her eyes for a second while pushing the cane, her arm could be hacked off before she was pulled through the merciless grinders. Guests at sugar plantations often remarked on how many one-armed people they saw.

Day after day, week after week, month after month, the cane was cut, hauled to the mill, and fed through the rollers. The mills kept going as long as there was cane to grind—the season varied between four and ten months, depending on the local growing conditions. A visitor who came to Brazil in 1630 described the scene: "People the color of the very night, working briskly and moaning at the same time without a moment of peace or rest, whoever sees all the confused and noisy machinery . . . will say that this indeed is the image of Hell."

A stream of pale ash-colored syrup gushed out from the mills, bubbling white with foam. The liquid rushed down a wooden gutter directly into the boiling house, a building of massive furnaces and cauldrons, where the syrup was heated and strained and turned into crystals. A giant copper kettle—often about four feet across and three feet deep—waited for the pale river. This was the first in a series of ever-smaller cauldrons, and beneath each gaped what the Brazilians called the "great open mouths"—the huge furnaces that had to be constantly filled with the wood that workers had chopped down and hauled to be ready for this moment. The boiling house was as perilous as the mills, for if a person nodded off for a second, he or she could slip into a bubbling vat.

Mammoth fires burned in the "mouths," clouds of steam billowed above the kettles, and the heat was so intense that the boiling houses had to be sprayed with water so they would not go up in flames. Then there was the smell, or rather, the stench of the boiling liquid. As the juice boiled, a foul scum rose to the top—which a slave had to keep skimming off with a long-handled ladle. Over and over again the liquid had to be strained and purified, even as it kept boiling, boiling, boiling in the copper vats.

Watching over the bubbling liquid was the "boiler"—a highly skilled slave. He judged each step, deciding when to pour the juice from one kettle to another, when it was ready for the next stage. His work led to one precise moment: when the syrup was so thick, and yet clean, that it was time to "strike." This was when the syrup was taken off the fire to cool so that it formed into crystals—grains of sugar. A master of striking was like a chemist or a winemaker, but also a kind of magician. He had to know the color, the smell, the feel of the boiling liquid so well, he could almost taste in the air that it was ready, just now.

Finally, sugar was a pile of crystals. But this was not the end: The crystals needed to be purified again, and depending on how carefully this was done, the end result could be dark brown, any one of many shades of lighter brown, or pure white. In Brazil, the crystals sat out for a month to dry, watched over by the "mothers of the platform"—enslaved women who knew how to tend the grains carefully, separating out the purest, whitest sugar from less valuable brown granules.

———

# PORTRAIT GALLERY OF SUGAR WORK

Sugar plantations were farms, but they had to run like factories—with human beings as the tireless machines. The lives of sugar workers were ruled by the cane, and by the relentless pace of work. Whether you look at drawings of sugar plantations made in the 1800s or at photographs taken a hundred years later, you see groups of poor people, an overseer seated above them on a horse, and the same steps in the sugar cycle. The following pages are like a slide show: a portrait gallery of sugar work.

William Clark visited the island of Antigua in the 1830s and painted the steps in making sugar. First the Africans prepared the ground (1): each cane cutting needed a space exactly five inches deep and five feet square. (2) (Courtesy St. Croix Landmarks Society and Archives)

A French artist visiting the island of Martinique around the same time as Clark showed a row of African women and men preparing the ground. (3) (Alcide Dessalines díOrbigny, Voyage Pittoresque dans les Dues Ameriques, facing p. 22, fig 4. Special Collections, University of Virginia)

When the crop was ripe, everyone worked on the harvest—even young children helped their mothers to bundle the cane. (4) (Courtesy St. Croix Landmarks Society and Archives)

As cane was cut, it had to be fed into the mill. (5) (Courtesy St. Croix Landmarks Society and Archives)

This drawing from the June 9, 1849, *Illustrated London News* gives a closer view of grinding —if your hand slipped, the wheels would pull you in; the sword propped next to the woman feeding the mill would be her only chance, as she could cut off her arm and save her life. (6) (Library of Congress)

The cane mash flowed to the boiling house, which was hot, foul smelling, and dangerous. (7) (Courtesy St. Croix Landmarks Society and Archives)

After the cane cooled into crystals, it was packed into hogsheads, to be shipped to eager customers. (8) (Courtesy St. Croix Landmarks Society and Archives)

4

## THE LAND OF THE SUGAR CANE.

In the West Indies, where the Sun
   With Tropic fervour heats the ground,
The SUGAR CANE is chiefly grown
   (Though 'tis in other regions found)

The earliest step is shown below,
Ere men begin the land to plough;
They burn the stubble, here called " Trash,"
And spread upon the soil its ash.

### PLANTING THE SUGAR CANE.

Now negroes " open up " the ground,
   And plant the Cane in square-shaped holes ;
     Meanwhile the Planter walks around
   With eagle glance, and all controls.
     The Hoeing, Watering, must
      ensue,
     To make the Cane crop
      thrive and grow.

The Cane is ripe, and men proceed
   To cut it down and strip the leaves.
All hands are pressed, and work with speed.
   A cart the welcome load receives.
It now is ready for the Mill,
Who's click-clack echoes o'er
   the hill.

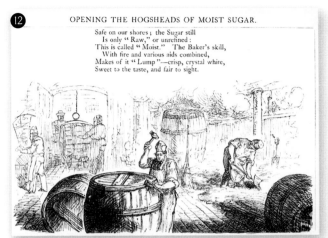

**12** OPENING THE HOGSHEADS OF MOIST SUGAR.

Safe on our shores ; the Sugar still
Is only " Raw," or unrefined :
This is called " Moist." The Baker's skill,
With fire and various aids combined,
Makes of it " Lump "—crisp, crystal white,
Sweet to the taste, and fair to sight.

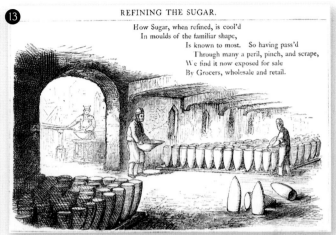

**13** REFINING THE SUGAR.

How Sugar, when refined, is cool'd
In moulds of the familiar shape,
Is known to most. So having pass'd
Through many a peril, pinch, and scrape,
We find it now exposed for sale
By Grocers, wholesale and retail.

**14** THE GROCER'S SHOP.

The Grocer's shop 's a human hive,
    Of honeyed goods from many a
    land ;
A part the grocer eats, to live ;
    The rest he shares with liberal
    hand.
The POUND OF SUGAR tarries here,
And waits your purchase, Reader,
    dear.

———

FINIS.

*The History of a Pound of Sugar,* a children's book published in England in 1861, showed the exact same stages that Clark depicted: preparing the fields (9); planting (10); harvesting (11); opening the hogsheads (12); refining the sugar (13); and selling sweets (14). Though aimed at young readers, the book makes clear the toil that brought sweets across the ocean. (COURTESY THE BALDWIN LIBRARY OF HISTORICAL CHILDREN'S LITERATURE, UNIVERSITY OF FLORIDA)

We see similar workers and more of the stages in the process in this and the following pages of photographs.

Two sugar workers are shown in this photo taken on the island of St. Kitts in 1901. (15) (LIBRARY OF CONGRESS)

The field is burned to clear away leaves and prepare the harvest near Guanica, Puerto Rico. (16) (LIBRARY OF CONGRESS) [THIS PHOTOGRAPH WAS TAKEN IN 1942 BY JACK DELANO, WHO WAS WORKING WITH THE ANTHROPOLOGIST SIDNEY MINTZ, WHOSE WORK SHAPED THE WRITING OF THIS BOOK.]

As ever, the foreman watches from his horse—taken near Manati, Puerto Rico, by Jack Delano. (17) (LIBRARY OF CONGRESS)

The large, clumsy stalks have to be hauled to the mills. This cart was being filled in Hawaii in 1917. (18) (LIBRARY OF CONGRESS)

The cane bunched and ready to be cut near New Iberia, Louisiana. (19) (LIBRARY OF CONGRESS)

Cutting the cane near Ponce, Puerto Rico. This photograph was taken in 1938 by Edwin Rosskam. (20) (LIBRARY OF CONGRESS)

The picture below was taken in 2005 in the sugar cane fields near San Jose de Los Llanos in the Dominican Republic. Life for sugar workers, such as these children and their parents, is very similar to what was shown in the previous photos. The hours are long, the pay is low, and the work is dangerous. And the workers get a lot of their calories from the cane itself. For these children—like the two boys in 1901 on page 7—sugar is food, not a treat. (21) (COURTESY UNCOMMON PRODUCTIONS)

21

The cut cane goes to the boiling house. This photograph was taken somewhere in the Caribbean and is damaged, but the burn almost seems to come from the heat of the syrup. (22) (LIBRARY OF CONGRESS)

22

In New Iberia, Louisiana, a boiler stands over a steaming vat. (23) (LIBRARY OF CONGRESS)

23

A modern sugar factory in Brazil. (24) (COURTESY LUANA RIBERIA DOS SANTOS)

24

Farmers near Guanica, Puerto Rico —where Jack Delano took several of the sugar harvest pictures— playing at a holiday party. Music can give us a hint of the lives and experiences of sugar workers. (LIBRARY OF CONGRESS)

## THE PULSE OF SUGAR LIFE

No one interviewed the Africans who labored in the sugar fields to ask them about their hard labor. They were meant to work and die. But there is one way we can hear them. The Africans invented music, dances, and songs that carry on the pulse, the beat, of their lives. (To hear examples of music from the sugar lands, go to www.sugarchangedthe world.com.) In Puerto Rico, bomba is a form of music and dance that the sugar workers invented. It is a kind of conversation in rhythm involving a woman, the man dancing with her, and the drummers who watch her and find the right rhythm for her movements. A master coming by would see dancing—no words of anger or rebellion. But as she moved and swayed, as the drummers "spoke" back in their beats, the workers were saying that they were not just labor, not just bodies born to work and die. Instead, they were alive and speaking to one another in movements and sounds that were all their own.

In Cuba, sugar workers told their stories in the words and sounds of rumba. As one song said, "The boss does not want me to play the drum."

Overseers feared the slaves were using drums to send messages and spread thoughts of rebellion.

Similarly, in Brazil there is a dance called Maculelê, which some trace to the sugar fields. Maculelê is danced with sticks or sugar cane stalks, and it looks very much like training for combat. On many of the sugar islands, Africans created similar dances in which people spin, jump, and seem to menace each other, then, just on the beat, click sticks and twirl away. The dances were a way of imitating warfare without actually defying the master.

Some of the enslaved took the next step. Running away from the sugar plantations, or attacking them in force, was another kind of statement. When the enslaved Africans could not stand their lives anymore, they risked everything to run or to fight. There was just one way for the owners to silence their workers: by making the price of flight or rebellion too high. Spreading terror was the job of the overseer.

Painted on the island of Dominica in 1779, this illustration shows stick fighting. Like Maculelê in Brazil, stick fighting was a contest, but also a way enslaved people could express themselves. They were not directly challenging their masters, but they were showing their skill and strength to each other.
(AGOSTINO BRUNIAS, JOHN CARTER BROWN LIBRARY AT BROWN UNIVERSITY)

# Palmares: The Maroon Kingdom

Zumbi—the name sounds like *zombie,* and that is exactly how many white Brazilians saw him. Zumbi followed his uncle Ganga Zumba (Great Lord) as the leader of the nation that escaped African, Native American, and even white slaves, created and defended in Brazil for nearly a century. He was a hero to his people and a terror to the European slave holders. Today Brazilians honor him as a great ancestor.

Between 1600 and 1695, Palmares (which means "place of the palm trees"), in the mountains behind Brazil's coastal sugar plantations, was a country unto itself. Europeans reported seeing workshops, blacksmiths, and potters, as well as well-defended cities with churches and meetinghouses.

At its peak, some 20,000 to 30,000 people lived in Palmares, following laws and customs in which beliefs brought over directly from Africa mixed with Native American and European practices. For example, they wore European clothes, decorated at times in African ways. They worshiped in Christian churches, in ceremonies that honored African gods. Most probably they cooked African yams in stews with European spice mixtures and native maize. Any slave on a Brazilian sugar plantation knew that freedom was close at hand—if he or she could make it to the mountains and join the community of Palmares.

Slaves who ran away and lived beyond the control of the planters were called "maroons"—from the Spanish word *cimarrón* for cattle that escaped and lived in the wild. Palmares was just the most visible example of the maroon communities that existed in all the sugar lands. Slaves would run away into the forest in the Guianas, to "cockpit country"—the steep canyons of Jamaica—to the swamps in North America. The planters did their best to wipe out maroon groups, but many were so strong and well defended that the Europeans signed peace treaties with them. The descendants of some maroon communities still live on the lands that the sugar lords never managed to conquer.

John Gabriel Stedman came to the Dutch sugar colony of Surinam in 1772 to fight against escaped slaves. He later wrote about his experiences and commissioned artists to depict the scenes he described. Here is a maroon fighter as shown in Stedman's work. (University of Amersterdam Library [UvA] Special Collections UBM: NOK 95-158, pl.2, t.o.p. 43)

James Hakewill drew this picture of the Cardiff Hall Great House in Jamaica in 1825. Built on a hill, the house was cooled by breezes and allowed the planter to look over his estate. Yet planters returned to England as soon as they could afford to, leaving the Great Houses behind. (JAMES HAKEWILL: A PICTURESQUE TOUR IN THE ISLAND OF JAMAICA, PLATE 23 SHELFMARK 1486.GG.11 BRITISH LIBRARY)

## THE OVERSEER

Thomas Thistlewood was twenty-nine when he arrived in Jamaica in 1750. At the time, about 17,000 people who were considered white lived there, and another 7,000 people were called "free blacks" or "coloreds"— they were people of mixed background who had some money or legal rights. The rest of the population, some 170,000 people, were enslaved workers, many of whom had been born in Africa and only recently sold into slavery. An overseer like Thomas needed to be so terrifying that the slaves who worked for him would never risk either fighting against him or running away. He needed to be sure that people feared his cruelty more than they craved freedom. As Equiano explained, "These overseers are indeed for the most part persons of the worst character of any denomination of men in the West Indies." That was true, but only half true, since the power of the overseers was a result of the curious lives led by the sugar masters.

The owner of a sugar plantation built a home—called the Great House—usually high on a hill, where the tropical breezes blow. The open windows provided a kind of air conditioning, making even the hottest days more pleasant. These grand homes, with their high, cool rooms, their polished mahogany furniture, their servants flitting between the main house and the separate cooking building, were meant to command attention, to show power and wealth. A plantation owner was a kind of god or king, ruling over his empire of sugar.

In the Great House the owners could sit on the verandahs, rest their legs on special chairs made for pulling off high rubber boots, drink their rum swizzlers, while their slaves labored on hundreds and hundreds of acres of cane fields. The furniture was imported from abroad, along with all the other comforts—silverware, silk-covered chairs, white christening gowns, porcelain washing bowls.

To this day, you can find the Great Houses of old plantations on hilltops throughout the Caribbean, and yet the strange thing is that the men who built and owned the homes hardly used them. For as soon as a sugar planter made enough money, he took his family and moved back to Europe. You can find the planters in the great English novels of the 1800s, such as Jane Austen's *Mansfield Park*, settled into their English homes and watching, through their account books, how the sugar crop was doing back in the Caribbean. While the masters enjoyed the life of wealth in Europe, the daily routine of the plantations was left in the hands of the overseers. Most often poor men who came to the New World to make their fortunes, the overseers had not the slightest sympathy for their enslaved workers.

Thistlewood learned the lesson of terror early on: He witnessed a master who had caught a runaway first whip him, then rub pepper, salt,

and lime into his wounds. That kind of cruelty was the norm in Jamaica. Thistlewood called it "pickling" and did it often. Indeed, masters kept going further, beyond all bounds of humanity. Thistlewood watched and learned. When he determined that a slave deserved punishment, he experimented with new forms of torture. For example, to punish one slave he "gagged him; locked his hands together; rubbed him with molasses & exposed him naked to the flies all day, and to the mosquitoes all night." But even that was not the worst of it.

If Thistlewood came to care for anyone, it was Phibbah, the enslaved woman he lived with for many years and freed in his will. But he had absolute power over his slaves, male and female. So he took any woman he wanted. By his own count, he was involved with 138 enslaved women. Neither the women nor their husbands, brothers, or parents had any

While masters built Great Houses that they hoped not to use, a slave's whole life fit into one room. This drawing of a slave "house" in Jamaica in 1823 appeared in a book defending slavery, so the artist made the scene look as clean, neat, and calm as possible. (CRYNRIC WILLIAMS, A TOUR THROUGH JAMAICA IN 1823; SHELFMARK 1050.1.24 BRITISH LIBRARY)

This image of a slave chained by the neck and the master holding a whip captures the reality of the Caribbean sugar plantations. The lithograph was made in the late 1700s by Friedrich Campe, a German artist who may have been telling us a second story: The slave is physically strong and looks like a recognizable human being. The master is pale and bloodless, as if he were more a wraith or vampire than a person. That is not far from the world Thomas Thistlewood describes in his diary.
(DER NEGER IN WESTINDIEN; PRINTS AND PHOTOGRAPHS, HOWARD UNIVERSITY LIBRARY)

choice in the matter. Those relationships were the real evil of the sugar plantation: A master could do anything he wanted, and a slave could not resist. That was the essence of sugar Hell.

Equiano reported that the sugar workers sometimes managed to harvest a bit of "grass" (sugar cane) to sell in the local market. But "nothing is more common than for the white people on this occasion to take the grass from them without paying." The slave had no rights; the masters had no fear. Worse yet, men would assault the women trying to make a bit of money, leaving them "poor, wretched, and helpless."

Sugar plantations were Hell because of the endless labor they demanded from slaves. They were Hell because of the many dangers and the injuries that they caused. They were Hell because the slaves who labored without end got nothing for their work—except to live another day, to work more. But none of these miseries was the true reason the plantations were so evil. The plantations were Hell because the masters and overseers were treated as gods—which turned them into devils. The English historian Lord Acton famously said, "Power tends to corrupt, and absolute power corrupts absolutely." That is a perfect description of sugar Hell. Men with absolute power over their slaves acted like creatures we would otherwise meet only in nightmares. Their cruelty had no limit—they preferred to kill their slaves rather than fear them. As Equiano explained, the island of Montserrat "requires 20,000 new Negroes annually, to fill up the vacant places of the dead."

To understand the slavery that brought Africans to the New World, you must begin with the death rate on the sugar plantations. Though we often think of slavery as a problem peculiar to the United States, only 4 percent of the slaves taken from Africa were brought to North America—which means that 96 percent went to the Caribbean, Brazil,

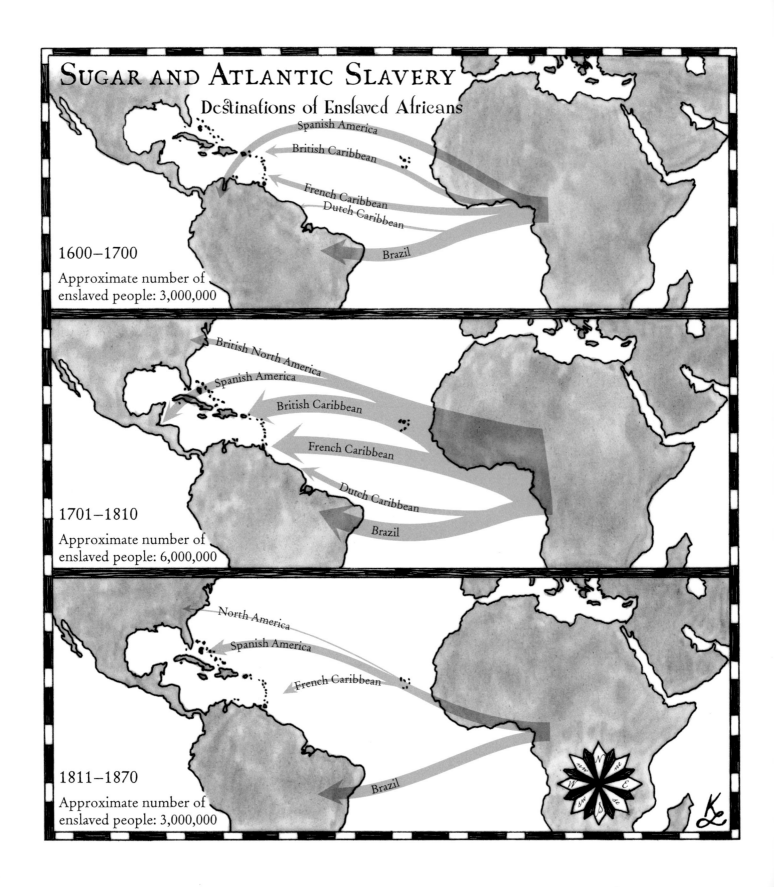

# Sugar and Atlantic Slavery

## Destinations of Enslaved Africans

Spanish America
British Caribbean
French Caribbean
Dutch Caribbean
Brazil

**1600–1700**

Approximate number of
enslaved people: 3,000,000

British North America
Spanish America
British Caribbean
French Caribbean
Dutch Caribbean
Brazil

**1701–1810**

Approximate number of
enslaved people: 6,000,000

North America
Spanish America
French Caribbean
Brazil

**1811–1870**

Approximate number of
enslaved people: 3,000,000

and the rest of South America, mostly to work with sugar. The slave population in North America grew over time as parents lived long enough to have children. Some 500,000 slaves were brought here, and there were four million enslaved African Americans at the time of emancipation. But on the sugar islands, while more than two million people were brought over from Africa, there were only 670,000 at emancipation. Sugar, with its demand for relentless labor, was a killer.

All this death, all this cruelty, all this abuse was for one purpose: to produce "white gold."

## BACK IN EUROPE

Remember Henry III and his difficulties in finding even a few pounds of sugar? Once Columbus brought sugar cane to the New World, that time was over. Sugar flooded from the islands back to Europe.

In 1565, at the wedding of a Portuguese princess and an Italian nobleman in Brussels, a long table displayed fruits from around the world, each one covered with a simple syrup made with sugar; the fruits from Europe, Africa, and the East Indies sat on plates with matching knives, and between them were chandeliers—every single item made from carved sugar. In another room was an even longer table on which figurines depicted the princess traveling on a ship past familiar locations, accompanied by whales, dolphins, and sea monsters. Some three thousand carved pieces of sugar stood on that table, showing every step of her trip, down to carved sugar birds in sugar cages and sugar elephants on parade.

Sugar was now the perfect decoration for a royal wedding, to be used

Pope Clement IX (on the right) served a banquet for the visiting Queen Christina of Sweden on December 9, 1668. The table was filled entirely with sculptures made out of sugar, as this watercolor drawing by Pierre Paul Sevin shows. (KUNGLIGA BIBLIOTEKET, STOLKHOLD; SHELFMARK H.UTS.B.89)

as lavishly as possible. But rich people will always find ways to show off their wealth—as the Muslim rulers had done with their sugar sculptures hundreds of years earlier. The real power of sugar depended on another substance: wrinkled leaves grown in the fields of Assam in northern India and all over China—tea.

## "The Best Sort of Chaw"

In 1615, Mr. Wickham, an Englishman, wrote to Mr. Eaton, a friend working for the East India Company in Japan, asking if he would be so kind as to buy him "a pot of the best sort of chaw." What he called "chaw" was tea—and this is the first time the drink was mentioned by a European. The only Europeans who knew tea were those few who worked in India, China, or Japan. Portugal controlled the trading city of Bombay, so the Portuguese had a head start in enjoying the drink. And when, in 1662, England's Charles II married Catherine of Braganza, a Portuguese princess, she brought Bombay as part of her dowry, and a taste for tea to the English court.

What the king and queen did was soon copied. The managers of the East India Company bought 20,000 pounds of tea in 1687, confident the firm could sell the leaves in England. The merchants were right. By 1711, the company was shipping 200,000 pounds of tea a year to England, and just forty years later, that had reached three million pounds. Told by their doctors that tea was good for their health, the English were drinking up to fifty cups a day. And yet, by the 1770s, the 1.75 million North Americans were actually drinking even more tea than the five to six million English. And with every cup of tea came several spoonfuls of sugar.

Tea is generally served warm and can have any one of many pleasant or enticing scents. But by itself tea is usually bitter, as were the two other new drinks that came to Europe in the 1600s—coffee and hot chocolate. The very first coffee shop in England was opened by a Turkish man in 1652. Outside of Europe, in places such as China, Arabia, and Mexico, people enjoyed their hot drinks plain. But in Europe, the three new drinks all invited the addition of sugar. And so by the 1700s, sugar was becoming a standard ingredient in England, Holland, and the North Americas for everyone who had a bit of money.

In the early 1700s, the average person in England consumed an estimated four pounds of sugar a year. A century later he was gulping down

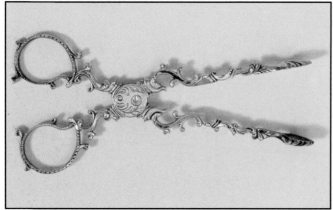

*Top left:* By 1727, when this picture was painted, a family in England showed off its wealth and status by serving a proper tea—with carefully selected tools such as a sugar dish, tea canister, and sugar tongs. (RICHARD COLLINS, "A FAMILY OF THREE AT TEA," V&A IMAGES/VICTORIA AND ALBERT MUSEUM)

*Bottom left:* Made in 1750, these silver "sugar nippers" were used to cut off a single serving of sugar from the larger loaf in which it was sold. As in the portrait, sugar was becoming a necessary household item for those eager to display their wealth and taste. (V&A IMAGES/ VICTORIA AND ALBERT MUSEUM)

*Right:* By the middle of the 1800s, any proper English home was supposed to have dishes for serving tea with sugar several times a day. This illustration is from Mrs. Beeton's cookbook, which was published in 1861 and became the standard source for English housewives. (BRITISH LIBRARY SHELFMARK 7942.DD.9.1318)

eighteen pounds. In one hundred years, the amount of sugar an English person used had increased by 450 percent. And that was before sugar really took off.

From the 1750s on, sugar transformed how Europeans ate. Chefs who served the wealthy began to divide meals up. Where sugar had previously been used either as a decoration (as in the wedding feast) or as a spice to flavor all courses, now it was removed from recipes for meat, fish, and vegetables and given its own place—in desserts. Dessert as the extremely sweet end to the meal was invented because so much sugar was available. But the wealthy were not the only ones whose meals were changing. Sugar became a food, a necessity, and the foundation of the diet for England's poorest workers.

Traditionally, English workers had brewed their own beer, which they drank along with bread, their other major source of food. A Scottish writer of the late 1700s noticed that tea had "become an economical substitute to the middle and lower classes of society for malt liquor," which they could no longer afford. "Tea," which had to be transported from Asia, and "sugar brought from the West Indies . . . compose a drink cheaper than beer." The new drink soon became not only cheap but necessary.

Why did the English, in particular, need a low-cost, filling hot drink? In a word: factories. England was the first country in the world to shift from making most of its money in traditional places, such as farms, mines, or small shops, to factories. In the early 1800s the English figured out how to build machines to weave cloth, and how to organize workers so that they could run the machines. Factory workers needed to leave their homes to go to work—they were not on farms where they could grow their own food, nor were they in shops where they could stop when they wanted to have a snack. Instead, they worked together in long shifts, taking breaks when allowed. Factory workers needed cheap food that was easy to transport and that gave them the energy to last until the next break.

All over England, in sooty cities such as Manchester and Liverpool, when the factory whistle blew, workers would set down their presses and file out to drink a quick cup of tea sweetened with sugar—usually dipping a piece of bread in the warm drink. Soon a smart manufacturer figured out that this break, and the need for a jolt of sweetness, was an opportunity. English workers were offered sugary cookies and candies—what we call today energy bars—that quick pick-me-up that helped workers to make it through their long shifts.

Starting around 1800, sugar became the staple food that allowed the English factories—the most advanced economies in the world—to run. Sugar supplied the energy, the hint of nutrition, the sweet taste to go with the warmth of tea that even the poorest factory worker could look forward to. Sugar was a necessity.

Why were the English the first to build factories to mill cloth? Because of the wealth they gained, the trade connections they made, and the banking systems they developed in the slave and sugar trade. Indeed, the cheap cloth from the factories was used to clothe the slaves. English factories, you might say, were built, run, and paid for by sugar.

In 1800, when the English were consuming

In this 1837 George Cruikshank illustration of a book by Charles Dickens, tea sweetened with sugar is sold on the streets of London. Sugar has changed from a luxury item to an absolute necessity. (BRITISH LIBRARY SHELFMARK G 18068 OPPOSITE 55)

their eighteen pounds of sugar a year, around 250,000 tons of sugar was produced worldwide—almost all sent to Europe. A century later, in 1900, when sugar was used in jams, cakes, syrups, and tea, and every modern country was filled with factories, world production of sugar reached six million tons. By that time, the average person in England ate ninety pounds of sugar a year—and in the early twentieth century, that number kept rising. (Americans today eat only about 40 pounds of cane sugar a year, but that is because other forms of sweeteners, such as corn syrup, are now cheaper than cane sugar. If you consider all forms of sweetener, Americans eat an average of 140 pounds every year.)

The first factories were places like this cotton weaving plant, drawn in England in 1835. Machines set the pace and workers could not choose when to stop. When they took a break, they needed a quick, cheap jolt of energy—which came in the form of sweet tea and cookies. The tea break was one of the ways the brutal sugar-slave world of the plantations and the new work rhythm of the industrial factory were linked. ("A Pair of Spinning Mules," British Library Shelfmark 1044.g.23 opposite 211)

———

# THE AGE OF SUGAR

By the 1800s, it was clear that the Age of Sugar—that combination of enslavement, factories, and global trade—was replacing the Age of Honey, when people ate local foods, lived on the land of their ancestors, and valued tradition over change. Sugar was the product of the slave and the addiction of the poor factory worker—the meeting place of the barbarism of overseers such as Thomas Thistlewood and the rigid new economy. And yet, for that very reason, sugar also became the lynchpin of the struggle for freedom.

When we talk about Atlantic slavery, we must describe sugar Hell; and yet that is only part of the story. Africans were at the heart of this great change in the economy, indeed in the lives of people throughout the world. Africans were the true global citizens—adjusting to a new land, a new religion, even to other Africans they would never have met in their homelands. Their labor made the Age of Sugar—the Industrial Age—possible. We should not see the enslaved people simply as victims, but rather as actors—as the heralds of the interconnected world in which we all live today. And indeed, it was when the enslaved Africans began to speak—in words and in actions—when Europeans began to see them as human, that the Age of Sugar also became the Age of Freedom.

# PART THREE

# Freedom

## ALL MEN ARE EQUAL

You could date a great change in the world to a visit one Madame Villeneuve made to France in 1714. That year, Pauline, an enslaved woman from the Caribbean, arrived in France as the personal servant of her mistress. When Madame Villeneuve set off from the coast to visit Paris, she left Pauline in a convent. The young woman spent her time studying with the nuns and went so far in her training that she asked to become a nun herself and remain in the convent. The nuns agreed, which enraged Madame

Villeneuve. She rushed to a judge, demanding to have her property back. Was Pauline a free woman, a bride of Christ, or an item to be bought, sold, and warehoused when she was not in use?

Twenty-three years earlier, King Louis XIV had issued a set of rules that defined slavery as legal in the French sugar islands. But when two slaves managed to reach France, he freed them—saying they became free "as soon as they [touched] the soil" of France. The judges sided with Pauline—she was real to them, human, not a piece of property. For Pauline's judges, as for King Louis, slavery far off across the seas was completely different from enslaved individuals in France.

Slave owners fought back, arguing that owners should be able to list their slaves as property when they arrived in France and take them with them when they left. Though most parts of France agreed to this, lawmakers in Paris hesitated. Pierre Lemerre the Younger made the case for the slaves. "All men are equal," he insisted in 1716—exactly sixty years before the Declaration of Independence.

To say that "all men are equal" in 1716, when slavery was flourishing in every corner of the world and most eastern Europeans themselves were farmers who could be sold along with the land they worked, was like announcing that there was a new sun in the sky. In the Age of Sugar, when slavery was more brutal than ever before, the idea that all humans are equal began to spread—toppling kings, overturning governments, transforming the entire world.

Sugar was the connection, the tie, between slavery and freedom. In order to create sugar, Europeans and colonists in the Americas destroyed Africans, turned them into objects. Just at that very same moment, Europeans—at home and across the Atlantic—decided that they could no longer stand being objects themselves. They each needed to vote, to speak out, to challenge the rules of crowned kings and royal princes. How could that be? Why did people keep speaking of equality while profiting from slaves? In fact, the global hunger for slave-grown sugar led directly to the end of slavery. Following the strand of sugar and slavery leads directly into the tumult of the Age of Revolutions. For in North America, then England, France, Haiti, and once again North America, the Age of Sugar brought about the great, final clash between freedom and slavery.

## All Men Are Equal: America

On Sunday evening, April 7, 1765, a swarm of Rhode Island men, their faces blackened, boarded the *Polly* and stripped the ship of its cargo: barrel after barrel of molasses from the sugar islands. This was eight years before the Boston Tea Party, but the issue was just the same. The British Parliament had placed a tax on sugar without giving the North Americans any voice in the matter, and the colonists were furious.

To the British, the Rhode Islanders who rolled the barrels off the ship so that they would not have to pay the sugar tax were smugglers, pure and simple. Yet the Americans claimed that they needed to resist the tax, or they would be mere slaves. A free man, the Americans believed, had the right to what he had built with his own strength, brains, and will. Sure, free men still needed to obey laws, but only if they had a say, a voice, in making those rules. Free men were not the silent, dutiful children of a wise king-father; rather, they were adults who spoke up for themselves. This was a major step away from the old Age of Honey— when a man's job was to be useful, obedient, and content with his lot in life. To the Americans, owning and controlling property was the difference between freedom and slavery. They would have resisted any tax, but sugar was an especially sore point.

The Caribbean planters who left their slaves in the hands of men like Thomas Thistlewood took full advantage of living in England. For by being near London, they could use their wealth to influence members of Parliament, and could even run for office themselves. William Beckford, for example, came from a family that owned twenty-four sugar plantations in Jamaica. As an adult he lived in England while owning two thousand people on the distant island. Known as Alderman Sugar-Cane, he was so successful that he became the mayor of London and a member of Parliament. Sugar lords like Beckford wanted to make sure American colonists would buy only from their islands, and would not be able to look for cheaper sugar elsewhere.

William Beckford, the lord mayor of London, owed his fortune to his sugar plantations in Jamaica. Americans were intensely aware of the power that the sugar lords wielded in London. (LIBRARY OF CONGRESS)

This image of one of Beckford's Jamaican estates was published in 1778. Clearly the artist, George Robertson, wanted it to look peaceful and beautiful, and to make slaves look meek and humble. (LIBRARY OF CONGRESS)

In North America, farmers plowing the rocky New England soil, or even the proud Virginians with their slave-run tobacco farms, did not have the luxury of turning their work over to others and moving to London. The Americans wanted cheap sugar and to be able to buy it anywhere, but they had no voice in Parliament. That made it extremely hard to take when Parliament sided with the sugar planters. Americans felt they were being cheated, silenced—in fact, enslaved.

In 1733, Parliament ruled that an extra six cents must be added to the price of every gallon of molasses that did not come from an English source. If the colonists actually followed the rules of the Molasses Act, it would have terrible consequences. Molasses from French islands would now be too expensive—merchants could never make a profit. So they would have to turn to the English, who would surely raise their prices. This one law could cripple the entire North American trade with the sugar islands—if, that is, the colonists or the French followed the rules. But of course they did just the opposite.

The Molasses Act accomplished nothing except to make Americans better smugglers. Yet the act was renewed again and again—until the crucial year of 1763. Just as the Molasses Act was due to expire, England completed its victory over France in the global contest known as the Seven Years' War (the segment of that war fought in North America is often called the French and Indian War). To pay for the war, the prime minister decided to put some teeth into the legislation. Now called the Sugar Act, the law was designed to make sure the American colonists stopped smuggling and paid their sugar tax.

As news of the toughened Sugar Act reached the North American colonists, they reacted with outrage—to them, this move by Parliament was precisely "taxation without representation." In Boston, the General Assembly responded by saying, "If Taxes are laid upon us . . . without ever having a Legal Representative where they are laid, are we not reduced from the Character of Free Subjects to the miserable status of Tributary Slaves?" Soon assemblies in New York and North Carolina joined the chorus, protesting against the Sugar Act.

When Parliament listened to the sugar lords, the colonists felt helpless, as if they were slaves. If England could take an American's property, he was not a free man. And so when Thomas Jefferson, with John Adams and Benjamin Franklin, wrote the Declaration of Independence, he insisted that there were certain rights no man could ever lose: life, liberty, and property (which is part of what "pursuit of happiness" meant). But, while Jefferson thought of slavery as an evil that he hoped would eventually disappear, he still believed in his own right to buy and sell slaves.

In the Age of Sugar, Americans gave their lives to defend what they owned, yet they continued to own other people. Paradoxically, it took the English to challenge the idea that a person could be bought and sold.

And it all began with a school assignment.

## "Is It Lawful to Make Slaves of Others Against Their Will?"

Each year Cambridge University gave a prize for the best essay written in Latin. This was no obscure test for a few scholars—winning the prize was considered a great honor. In 1785, the man who chose the subject for the contest decided to use it as a weapon against slavery, so he asked the contestants to respond to the question "Is it lawful to make slaves of others against their will?" Thomas Clarkson was so good at Latin that he won the prize. His goal was just to write a winning essay, but in the process he convinced himself. "A thought came into my mind, that if the contents of the Essay were true, it was time some person should see these calamities to their end."

Once Clarkson realized that every second of every day human lives were being destroyed and he was letting it happen, he changed the course of his life—risking everything to abolish this terrible practice. As he explained, "In the day-time I was uneasy. In the night I had little rest. I sometimes never closed my eye-lids for grief."

The English public, now consuming some eighteen pounds of sugar a year, knew little about the lives of the enslaved Africans whose labor sweetened their meals. Worse yet, every Englishman who hammered the wood, sewed the sails, manufactured the rope for slave ships, or built the barrels to hold slave-harvested sugar made his money from the slave trade. The English were getting richer because Africans were being turned into property. Clarkson and others who believed as he did, who in the coming decades would be called abolitionists, realized that while that link gave the English a stake in slavery, it also gave the antislavery forces an opportunity. If they could reverse the flow—make the horrors of slavery visible to those who benefited from it—they might be able to end the vile practice forever.

The abolitionists were brilliant. They created the most effective public relations campaign in history, inventing techniques that we use to this day. When he spoke, Clarkson brandished whips and handcuffs used on slaves; he published testimonials from sailors and ship doctors who described the atrocities and punishments on slave ships. When Olaudah Equiano published his memoir, he educated his readers about the horrors of the slave trade. And then, when the English began to understand what slavery really was, Clarkson and others organized what we would call a boycott of "the blood-sweetened beverage."

Slave labor was valuable because it produced cheap sugar that everyone wanted to buy. But if people stopped buying that sugar, the whole slave system would collapse. In the years leading up to the American Revolution, the women of New England refused to buy English products and English tea. The loss of income made London rescind some of the taxes it had imposed on America. Now this same tactic—boycotting—was used to fight slavery. Some 400,000 English people stopped buying the sugar that slaves grew and harvested. Instead, they bought loaves of sugar that carried a label that said, "Produced by the labour of FREEMEN"—the sugar came from India.

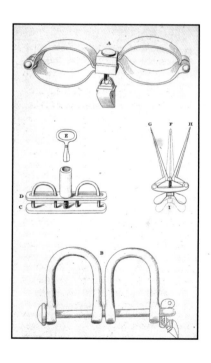

This illustration showing the tools used to punish and torture slaves appeared in Olaudah Equiano's autobiography. He spoke of how even slave masters were hardened by the cruelty of the trade, and his readers saw visible evidence as they turned the pages. (BRITISH LIBRARY SHELFMARK 522.F.23. VOL I)

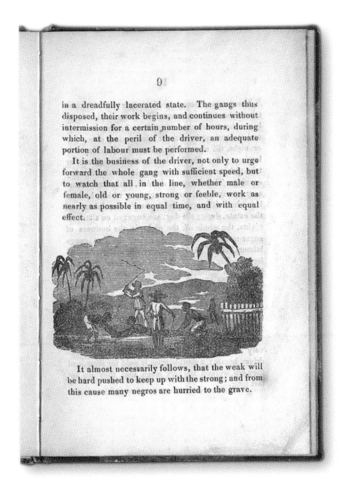

The abolitionists were brilliant at using advertising and marketing to turn public opinion against slavery. A pamphlet written by the Peckham Ladies African and Anti-Slavery Association urged readers to use sugar only from India. (BRITISH LIBRARY SHELFMARK 8155.1.21)

When the English looked at the sugar they used every day, Clarkson and the other abolitionists made them see the blood of the slaves who had created it. The very fact that slave-made sugar was so popular made it harder for the English to ignore the reality of slavery. Sugar was a bridge—like the sneakers and T-shirts and rugs that, today, we know are made by sweatshop labor. If you wanted the product, abolitionists

In 1826, Amelie Opie published a children's book aimed at exposing the horrors of sugar slavery. (BRITISH LIBRARY T.1271)

forced you to think about how it was made. Slavery—a practice as ancient as human civilization—was becoming unacceptable, a form of inhumanity people could no longer tolerate.

American colonists had gone to war when they felt the English were treating them as slaves, but they left the problem of their own slaves to be resolved later. Now some in England were speaking up for the actual slaves. And then the flame of revolution spread, to France.

## ALL MEN ARE EQUAL: FRANCE

In France, there was no Parliament or Congress; no one expected to be able to protect his rights by voting. But even in the land of King Louis XVI and Queen Marie Antoinette, the people demanded to be heard. In July 1789, Parisians stormed the Bastille, the hated prison where the king locked up anyone he disliked. And in August, the newly defined National Assembly issued the Declaration of the Rights of Man and the Citizen. "Men are born and remain free and equal in rights," it announced to the world. Here it was again, Pierre Lemerre's phrase, Jefferson's phrase, the principle Clarkson was fighting for—indeed, he came to France to support the new government. And yet the Declaration also said that "property is an inviolable and sacred right." So what were slaves? Equal human beings, or goods that belonged to their owners?

Human rights versus property rights. That argument goes on today as, for example, we debate how closely to regulate coal mining. Is it best to let owners set rules, which is likely to give all of us cheaper coal, or to have the government set standards, which is more likely to protect workers and the environment? In France, one side argued that slaves must be freed. The other said that to change anything in the sugar islands would invite slave revolts, help France's rivals, and thus hurt the nation.

At meetings of the Female Society of Birmingham, women gathered in sewing circles to make bags decorated with abolitionist images, such as the one below. While many abolitionist groups favored a gradual approach to ending slavery, the women of Birmingham read and discussed Elizabeth Heyrick's argument that all slaves must be freed at once. (V&A IMAGES/VICTORIA AND ALBERT MUSEUM)

This model shows how the anti-slavery bag would have been worn and displayed—shaming everyone who passed into thinking about the blood price of the sugar in their tea. (V&A IMAGES/VICTORIA AND ALBERT MUSEUM)

In the new United States, the Revolution gave white men with property a sense of freedom, while Africans were still enslaved. In England, abolitionists spoke up for Africans, but kings and lords still ruled. In France, revolutionaries were turning against their own nobles but remained uncertain about what this meant for enslaved Africans on their sugar islands. The Age of Revolutions was pressing ideas of freedom against the rights of property, and no one was sure where these great clashes would lead.

In revolutionary France, the defenders of slaves began to win the argument against the advocates of property rights. By fall of 1791, the French passed a law making free blacks and people of mixed background on the sugar islands legally equal to all other Frenchmen. Yet this was not good news for Clarkson and his allies in England. For even as the revolutionaries in France passed humane laws, they began using the guillotine to execute their own lords and nobles. As blood started to flow in the streets of Paris, slave owners in England and the Americas were given a perfect defense: If you interfere with property rights, if you free slaves, if you change anything in the government, the result will be chaos and terror.

By the 1790s, the English abolitionists were losing popularity, momentum, and hope. After all, the chaos in France made the English slave trade and sugar islands all the more profitable. And then a new voice began to be heard from the most profitable, slave-dominated sugar island of all, the very land to which Columbus had brought his first sugar plants.

## THE SOUND OF LIBERTY

By the late 1700s, Saint Domingue (what is now Haiti) was the world center of sugar. So many sugar plantations dotted the landscape that slaves called commanders managed other slaves. On the night of August 14, 1791, commanders from the richest sugar plantations in Saint Domingue gathered in a place called Alligator Woods and swore a solemn oath. They would rise up against their white owners, "and listen to the voice of liberty which speaks in the hearts of all of us." That voice told them to destroy everything related to sugar. Sugar made the Africans slaves, so sugar must be wiped off the island, now a vast sugar factory to the world.

By the end of August, the French colony was in flames. So many cane fields were on fire that the air was filled with "a rain of fire composed of burning bits of cane-straw which whirled like thick snow." Smashing mills, destroying warehouses, setting fields on fire, the freedom fighters demolished some one thousand plantations—and that was just in the first two months of their revolution. The fight against sugar and chains soon had a leader, Toussaint, who called himself "L'Ouverture"—the opening. Toussaint was making a space, an opening, for people to be free.

The enslaved people on Saint Domingue were not merely fighting against the terrible conditions on the island. They were fighting for principles that they had learned from Europeans and Americans—from people similar to their own slave masters. The trio of great principles behind the French Revolution that began in 1789 consisted of "liberty, equality, fraternity" (brotherhood). As boats arrived in Saint Domingue from France, slaves learned that a revolution was going on in the name of human rights. Already, they'd been given a taste of great change because of a revolution closer to home. In 1779, a regiment of free blacks from Saint Domingue went to America to join in the fight for independence. They brought home with them the idea that "all men are created equal."

Two years after the meeting in Alligator Woods, on August 29, 1793, the leading French official on Saint Domingue realized that there was no point in opposing Toussaint and his armies. The slaves had freed themselves. And the following February, Paris agreed. The ideal of brotherhood announced by the revolutionaries of Paris finally included the sugar workers of Saint Domingue.

With their victory, the people of Saint Domingue announced that the conflict between freedom and property was over: "All men are equal" meant that no men are property. This idea terrified the English—and not merely because their sugar island of Jamaica was just over a hundred miles across the water from Saint Domingue. Indeed, slaves in Jamaica were beginning to sing a new song while they worked:

> One, two, tree,
> All de same;
> Black, white, brown,
> All de same;
> All de same.
> One, two, tree,
> All de same!

That chant did more than threaten a slave revolt—it was a challenge to all ranking hierarchies. Jamaica had already seen many slave revolts,

This image celebrates the moment on July 7, 1801, when Toussaint accepted a constitution that gave him control of the entire island of Hispaniola. (LIBRARY OF CONGRESS)

Trelawney Town in Jamaica shows how threatening the Haitian revolt was to slaveholders everywhere. The village was run by maroons whom the British had been unable to defeat. In 1730 the British signed a peace treaty with the maroon leaders, but sixty years later, as former slaves fought for freedom in nearby Haiti, the English went back on their word, captured as many maroons as they could, and sent them to Canada. The descendants of maroons who evaded the British still live in Jamaica to this day. (REPRO ID E9983 NATIONAL MARITIME MUSEUM)

and the reverend John Lindsay was certain that the talk of freedom and liberty in North America had inspired the slaves: "At our tables (where . . . every Person has his own waiting man behind him) we have I am afraid been too careless of Expressions, especially when the topic of American rebellion has been . . . brandished with strains of Virtuous Heroism." But the slaves did not need to overhear their masters to learn about the ideas of equality. Black sailors working ships running all through the islands were carrying the word. And if this spirit of liberty got out of hand, that could be really dangerous. After all, in England itself only 3 percent of the population had the right to vote. If this expanded idea of freedom spread, how safe were the kings and dukes, earls and knights, of England? Starting in fall 1793, British troops began arriving in Saint Domingue to reenslave people and return them to their sugar plantations. As Henry Dundas, the British secretary of war, put it, their goal was to "prevent a circulation in the British Colonies of the wild and pernicious Doctrines of Liberty and Equality."

Liberty and equality—how far could these ideas spread? What could stand against them? Could any king hold on to his crown? Could any slave master keep his slaves? The English invaded to silence these questions, and they were sure they would easily win—after all, their army and navy were the best in the world, and they were fighting against mere ex-slaves.

But in fact, the Haitians were disciplined, smart fighters. One reason they did so well in battle is precisely because the slave trade was flourishing. Many of the Haitian soldiers were recently arrived Africans, warriors in their home countries. They were trained in military tactics, which they put to good use against the English. The English were also devastated by tropical diseases—malaria and yellow fever—which took thousands of lives. But in the end, the Haitians won because of the fire of their cause. As Toussaint neared the last British stronghold, he said, "We are fighting that liberty—that most precious of all earthly possessions—may not perish." Abraham Lincoln would use almost precisely the same words in his Gettysburg Address some sixty-five years later. By October 1798, the British gave up. But that did not mean Toussaint had won—he still faced two more powerful foes. The first was France—the very country that had inspired the Haitians and granted them their freedom. The second was fear.

Back in France, the government that had abolished slavery was in the process of destroying itself. The great paradox about the French Revolution is that even as the revolutionaries passed ever more laws to benefit the poor and enslaved, those same leaders turned increasingly zealous in murdering their enemies. This is like so many regimes in which, to this day, a tyrant claims he is helping the people while he jails his opponents and robs his nation. Great ideas cover up brutal behavior.

In 1799, Napoleon Bonaparte, the best general in France, put an end to the revolutionary bloodbath. He seized power and made his own new rules. Napoleon quickly recognized how important sugar was to his nation. First he reversed the law that had freed the slaves. Then he set about to create a sugar-and-slave empire for France that would rival England's. He made a deal with Spain that gave France control of the middle of North America, from New Orleans north along the Mississippi. Then he made peace with England and sent an army to crush the rebellious people of Saint Domingue. Once he regained control of the sugar island, he could use the Louisiana Territory to feed and supply all his sugar plantations in the Caribbean, and reap the rewards in white gold.

The great seesaw between freedom and property kept swinging. The United States of America broke free of England but kept slavery. France had freed slaves but then consumed itself in violence. England had begun talking about ending slavery, but then it saw the chaos in France and sent an army to try to defeat the Haitians. Now Napoleon's France followed in the footsteps of the English.

Napoleon's 35,000-man army was led by his brother-in-law and soon scored an amazing success: They captured Toussaint in 1802 and brought him to France, where he died in prison in 1803. But the former slaves fought on. In two years of fighting, nearly 50,000 French soldiers died. And on January 1, 1804, the victorious Republic of Haiti was born. Fighting for freedom, the former slaves defeated the armies of first England, then France: Europe's two most powerful nations.

Haiti was born free; human rights won over property rights. But the free people of Haiti still faced their last, and most devastating, opponent: fear.

The leaders of the American Revolution kept close watch as the former slaves fought for their freedom in Haiti. But that fight split the

Toussaint was captured by the French in 1802 and died in France. But the former slaves in what became Haiti defeated the French army. This image, created thirty years later, shows one of the many clashes in that war. In 1804 Haiti became the second nation in the Americas to become independent. (HISTORICAL MUSEUM OF SOUTHERN FLORIDA)

Founding Fathers—who had their own conflicts about how to deal with slavery in the new United States. When John Adams was president, he sent guns and supplies to Toussaint to help in the struggle against the French. Thomas Jefferson, though, was terrified by the success of the Haitian revolution.

When Thomas Jefferson succeeded Adams, he saw Haiti only as a threat. He expected ex-slaves from the island to spread into America, preaching freedom and rebellion to the slaves. "Unless something is done," he warned, "and soon done, we shall be the murderers of our own children . . . ; the revolutionary storm now sweeping the globe will be upon us." So he refused to recognize Haiti—America's only sister republic. In fact, it was not until 1862 that Abraham Lincoln, about to issue the Emancipation Proclamation, finally established relations with Haiti.

Americans like Jefferson were proud of having fought for their freedom. But as long as they could still see Africans as property, they could not treat Haitians as equally brave and courageous human beings. For if Haitians could claim their freedom and be recognized by America, why couldn't slaves within the United States do the same thing?

The great European powers were equally unwilling to recognize the land where slaves had freed themselves. Isolated in the world, without the benefit of trade and contact that would have come if other countries in the Americas or Europe had treated it as a partner, Haiti floundered. In part that was because of internal conflicts in which outsiders had no role. But Haiti never really recovered from its difficult birth. The country frightened slave owners; it did not change their views.

After 1804, the slaves of Haiti were free. But throughout the rest of the old sugar lands, cane was still growing, and slaves were still giving their lives to harvest it. Back in England, Clarkson and his friends saw their chance: France was no longer in the midst of a revolution, and Napoleon's sugar dreams had failed. England now had no excuse; the abolitionists would force their countrymen to face the question: Was England a nation built on Christian beliefs or on treating people as property?

In 1806, the antislavery forces brought a new bill before Parliament that would limit British involvement in the slave trade. Some of the most powerful testimony in favor of the bill came from former army officers who had been to the Caribbean and had seen the courage of the former slaves and the horrors of slavery. The slaves spoke through the testimony of the very men who had gone to fight them. One member of Parliament told his colleagues of the tortures he had seen in the islands. Slavery was not an abstraction, an economic force, a counter in the game of world politics—it was the suffering of men and women. Members of Parliament were being confronted with the reality of slavery, just as audiences at Clarkson's lectures were when he showed shackles and whips.

While Parliament debated the new bill, Clarkson and his allies went on lecturing, talking, changing minds all across England. They succeeded. Newspapers reported that even in Bristol, a port city with a harbor filled with slave ships, "the popular sentiment has been very strongly expressed against the continuance of that traffick in human flesh."

William Wilberforce, another leader of the abolitionist cause, felt the new mood in his country. "God can turn the hearts of men," he marveled. Many members of Parliament recognized the same change in the "sense of the nation." In 1807 a bill to ban all English involvement in slave trading passed the House of Commons, then the House of Lords. At precisely noon on March 25, King George III signed the law. We should mark that date, honor it, to this day. For while no slaves were freed by the bill, it marked a great change in the world. More slaves from Africa had been shipped by the British than by any other nation. That part of the grim history of sugar and slavery was over. Indeed, that very same year Congress passed a law forbidding Americans from being involved in importing slaves. In the great contest over whether a human, any human, could ever be property, the tide was turning. And yet the tangled story of slavery, sugar, and freedom still had one extremely dark twist to come, in the United States.

———————

This coin celebrates the first accomplishment of the abolitionists: ending the English slave trade in 1807. The coin was not actually minted until the 1830s, when it was used in Sierra Leone, the African colony designed for freed slaves. Whereas in England even abolitionists portrayed humble slaves on their knees pleading for freedom, in this coin designed for use in Africa, the English and the African are shown as nearly equal. (NATIONAL MARITIME MUSEUM)

## THE SUGAR PURCHASE AND THE DEATH STATE

In the 1930s, reporters spread out across the American South to capture the voices of history. Some African Americans who had been born as slaves were still alive, and could describe how they had lived sixty years earlier. Through their words we can finally begin to hear about sugar slavery from those who lived it.

Ellen Betts, who grew up as a slave on a sugar plantation in Louisiana, recalled that they worked "hour in, hour out, them sugar cane fields sure stretch from one end of the earth to the other." Ceceil George remembered that she "come up in hard times—slavery times." "Every body worked, young, an ole', if yo' could carry two or three sugar cane yo' worked. Sunday, Monday, it all de same . . . it like a heathen part o' de country." She meant that in other states slaves got Sunday off to worship God. Not in Louisiana: There, sugar was god, and work was the only religion.

When the Haitians defeated the French armies, Napoleon lost control of the world's most productive sugar islands and with it his dream of great sugar profits. As a result, Napoleon had no use for the land in North America he had so recently obtained from Spain. Napoleon did, though, need money to pay for his wars. That is why he sold the vast Louisiana Territory to Jefferson for the bargain price of just fifteen million dollars. What textbooks call the Louisiana Purchase should really be named the Sugar Purchase. Americans obtained the middle part of what would become their nation because the Haitians achieved their freedom. But, paradoxically, that gave Haitian slave owners a new home.

As sugar planters fled from the revolution in Haiti, some moved to Cuba's Oriente Province, others to North America—to Louisiana. By the time the Haitian plantation owners and overseers reached New Orleans, abolitionists were pressing to end the African slave trade. The tragedy is that this movement to end slavery did nothing to improve conditions in Louisiana. In fact, the state that slaves called Lousy Anna was the very worst place for an African in America; it was the Caribbean all over again—a death sentence.

In every single American slave state, the population of enslaved people kept rising even after the slave trade was abolished. That was because enough enslaved children were born, lived, and grew to become adults. There was just one exception to this rule: Louisiana, where the native-born enslaved population kept dropping. Sugar was a killer.

Unlike the Caribbean, Louisiana has cold snaps. That put an additional pressure on the sugar harvest. Not only did the slaves need to

This 1875 engraving of a sugar harvest in Louisiana shows the factory near the fields. Because sugar came to Louisiana late, it married the pace of the steam engine to the endless labor of the cane cycle. (LIBRARY OF CONGRESS)

harvest the cane in perfect rhythm with the grinding mills, but the entire crop had to be cut down between mid-October and December. This pace only increased when growers installed improved, steam-powered mills. People needed to work faster than the weather and to keep pace with machines.

We have a hint of this relentless life in the words left behind by former slaves. Ephraim Knowlton took over as a Louisiana estate manager in 1857, and he put everyone to work. The youngest children were organized into the "suckling gang" and sent out to weed the cane fields. Their older brothers and sisters, those who were eleven to fifteen, carried water out to everyone else who worked in the fields. Even those few older slaves who could no longer labor with cane, no matter how maimed or injured, had to repair tools or nurse the newly wounded.

Knowing that their slaves were likely to die by the time they reached their thirties, Louisiana sugar planters were extremely selective—they bought only healthy-looking young men in their late teens. On average, the men purchased in Louisiana were an inch taller than the people bought in the other slave states. Those teenagers made up seven to eight out of every ten slaves brought to America's sugar Hell. The others were younger teenage girls, around fifteen to sixteen years old. Their job, for the rest of their short lives, was to have children. Elizabeth Ross Hite knew that, for sure, "all de master wanted was fo' dem wimmen to hav children." Enslaved children would be put to work or sold. The overseer S. B. Raby explained, "Rachel had a 'fine boy' last Sunday. Our crop of negroes will I think make up any deficiencies there may be in the cane crop." That is, a master could sell any slaves who managed to live, if he needed more money than he could make from sugar.

Jazz was born in Louisiana. Could it be that a population of teenagers, almost all of them male, were inspired to develop their own music as a way to speak, to compete, to announce who they were to the world? Bomba in Puerto Rico, Maculelê in Brazil, jazz in Louisiana— all gave people a chance to be alive, to be human, to have ideas, and dreams, and passions when their owners claimed they were just cogs in machinery built to produce sugar. The sugar workers spoke in another way, too. In 1811, Charles Deslondes, a free person of color from Saint Domingue, led what is sometimes called the largest slave revolt in U.S. history. He gathered slaves to attack a plantation, then head down toward New Orleans. Met by troops composed of both blacks and whites, some sixty-six slaves were killed, as well as two whites. The rebellion failed. But it is a sign of the strong link between Louisiana and Haiti. Whites remembered their rule on the island; blacks remembered their fight for freedom.

The sugar story in the United States centered on Louisiana—though even supposedly free states like New York made fortunes in transporting and selling sugar grown by slaves. When the nation split during the Civil War, Northerners could no longer get cane from those plantations along the Mississippi, so they had to go across the ocean—to paradise: Hawaii.

## Sugar in Paradise: "I came seeking the dream"

Hawaii is where the two journeys of sugar cane join. Starting around 1100, the first inhabitants of Hawaii brought cane stalks with them on their long journey across the Pacific. So by the 1800s, when Europeans began to explore the islands, they saw lush green cane stalks already growing thickly from sea level up into the hills. As we have seen, the plant's westward journey took it from New Guinea to India, then on to Persia, the Middle East, the Mediterranean, and the Azores, then, via Columbus, to the New World. By the nineteenth century, when growers turned to the richly planted islands of Hawaii, they brought with them the knowledge of how to run sugar plantations. Now growers who knew all about plantations, mills, and refining found sugar waiting for them on islands as beautiful as Hispaniola had been when Columbus arrived.

But whom could they get to do the backbreaking sugar work? The United States was in the midst of the Civil War; slaves from Africa were not an option. So they looked to the east, to China.

In Hawaii, planters first brought men—only men—from China to work the crop. In the 1850s, Chinese workers were not well paid, but neither were they slaves. The more Chinese came, the more they began to want better wages and conditions. To stop that dangerous idea, in the 1880s, growers turned to men from Japan. Just when the Japanese started to make demands, the United States won the Spanish-American War (in 1898) and took control of the Philippines. Now Filipino men were imported to the sugar fields to compete with the Chinese and Japanese. So too were Koreans and Portuguese. Ads were posted in Spain to attract sugar workers there; even a few African Americans came from the mainland.

Once again music and songs helped the sugar workers to keep up their spirits—to speak to one another in ways their bosses could not understand. When the Japanese men earned a bit of money, they wrote home, sending photos (which might really be of themselves, or might show someone younger or better-looking) to create a match with a "picture bride"—a woman who would send her photo to the islands. Slowly, Japanese women joined men on the sugar plantations.

Sugar work in Hawaii brought the same scene as took place in the Caribbean —the foreman on his horse, the gangs of workers harvesting the cane. But now the workers, male and female, were most often Asian. (Bishop Museum)

In the fields, Japanese women would sing *holehole bushi*—*holehole* is a Hawaiian word meaning "stripping leaves," and *bushi* is Japanese for "song." Even the term used for these songs was a blend, a sign of the mixing of lives on the islands. Some of the songs were funny, some sexy; some, like this one, remind us of Thomas Thistlewood and the terrible days of sugar Hell:

> *Earthquakes and thunder*
> *Do not scare me*
> *But a sound from the overseer*
> *Leaves me quaking*

The sugar workers in Hawaii were not enslaved—they chose to come. But they still lived hard lives:

> *Hawai'i, Hawai'i*
> *I came seeking the dream*
> *But my tears now flow*
> *In the canefields*

When the Africans were brought to work in sugar, they had to form new families, learn new languages—they had to find ways to blend their new lives with what they recalled from their homelands. The *holehole bushi* hint at one way sugar workers have always found strength and comfort:

> *My husband cuts the cane*
> *I carry the stalks from the field*
> *Together, the two of us*
> *We get by*

Because they could not use slaves, Hawaiian sugar growers turned to one ethnic group after another, trying to keep wages low by having each new type of worker compete with the old. But all this planning to create division had the strangest effect: It made Hawaii into the most ethnically diverse place in the world. So, in 1959, when Hawaii finally became a state, it was more like the multicultural land the United States was becoming than the sugar Hells that were so much a part of its history.

Sugar in Hawaii bridges east and west. And it finally brings us back to the story Marc learned in Israel and the one Marina found in Guyana. We return to our own stories just at the moment in history when we can finally, fully hear and see the sugar workers, and when the clash between human freedom and humans as property reached its great climax.

# PART FOUR

# Back to Our Stories:
# New Workers, New Sugar

## A New System

*British India, 1870s.*

It might begin at a fair. You're there to sell vegetables, to pick up a job for the day, or maybe just to enjoy the sights.

A stranger sidles up and whispers, "You want to make a better wage? There's good work upriver." Or he might buy you some roti (bread) and lentils, promise a new life, good money, enough to send back to your poor mother and father. Maybe there was another man (a decoy, but you don't know that) boasting of how rich you'll be soon

enough. And so you agree—you walk with the stranger along the hot, dusty roads, picking up other recruits, who hear the same story. If you balk or get suspicious, the slippery-tongued stranger cleverly responds: *Fine, but I have fed you for the past few days, and you must pay me back.* Of course, you have no money, so you walk on to take on this new work.

Sometimes he hints at where you are headed—"gone to Damra"(Demerara). The Demerara is a river in Guyana, but the word was also used to refer to a region, and even to the colony itself. So, no matter what the stranger says, you have no real idea of where you are going, or what you will be expected to do. In fact, among the immigrants, it was called "gone to Tapu," which was not a specific place. It meant something like "disappeared" or "vanished," and carried a hint of evil or danger.

This was called indenture: the new way to find people to work the sugar fields. And it took place thousands and thousands of miles away from the sugar islands—in India.

The seeds for this system were sown in 1823 in the sugar colony of British Guiana—now Guyana—where John Gladstone, father of the future British prime minister William Gladstone, owned over a thousand slaves. John Smith, a young and idealistic English preacher who had recently come to the area, was becoming popular with those slaves. His inspiring sermons retold the story of Moses leading the Jews out of Egypt and to freedom. The sugar workers listened and understood: Smith was speaking not about the Bible, but about the present. That summer, after hearing one of Smith's sermons, over three thousand slaves grabbed their machetes, their long poles, and rose up against their masters. The governor of the colony rushed toward the burning plantations, where he met a group of armed slaves, and asked them what they wanted.

"Our rights," came the reply. Here was Haiti—and for that matter America and France—all over again. The slaves insisted they were not property; like the Jews in Egypt, they were God's children, who were owed their basic human rights.

The English had stopped the slave trade, but the rulers of a sugar colony were not yet ready to listen to slaves demanding to be treated as full human beings. The governor called in his forces, who brutally put down the revolt. Rebellious slaves were chased through the fields, and if they fled into the nearby forests, troops hunted them down. Quamina, the alleged leader of the uprising, was hanged in chains in front of the entrance to one of Gladstone's plantations. And John Smith was tried and sentenced to be put to death in England—though he died of tuberculosis before his ship reached London.

News of the Reverend Smith's death provoked a huge outcry in British newspapers and in Parliament. Slavery depended on brutality—the death of a minister, an idealistic, white English minister, convinced more and more people in England that this was an immoral trade. And though the controversy did not immediately bring the abolition of slavery, the end was in sight.

The slavers had always been able to count on the support of English nobles, who resisted any change that might diminish their power. But even as the abolitionists spoke up for the rights of Africans, Parliament was finally seriously considering giving more English people the right to vote. It is as if the hands on a great national clock were moving together toward high noon. The old age of slavery overseas and a Parliament elected by only 3 percent of the English was ticking down to days, to hours, to minutes, to seconds. In 1833, exactly ten years after the terrible British Guianan rebellion, the Emancipation Bill was finally passed. England—royal, aristocratic, class-bound England—made slavery itself illegal. On August 1, 1838, all slaves would be freed. Clarkson, Wilberforce, and their fellow abolitionists had won. The Quaker William Allen, who had sworn off sugar for nearly fifty years while he battled against slavery, drank his first cup of tea with a spoonful of white, free sugar.

The end of slavery was a great step for human rights. But what did it mean on the sugar plantations—which had depended on extremely cheap labor to keep up with the twenty-four-hour cycle from harvest to mill? In 1836, the same John Gladstone whose sugar estate had exhibited the chained body of the slave leader Quamina wrote to a shipping company. Gladstone asked it to provide a hundred workers (the slang name was "coolies") from India to labor on his plantations. Gladstone's first ships, the *Whitby*, carrying 249 passengers, and the *Hesperus*, carrying 244, sailed for Demerara in 1838.

Thus began a new chapter in the story of sugar.

## CROSSING THE BLACK WATER

Why would any Indian risk going off to work in sugar? At the time, India was very, very poor, especially in the north, where famines and droughts had swept across the countryside and people were pushed off their land. Leaving home to find work was not a new idea. But there was a catch, a special problem, in sugar work. The people of India practiced many different religions: There were Muslims, Buddhists, Sikhs, Catholics, Parsees, Jains, even Indian Jews. But most Indians were Hindus. And for traditional Hindus, leaving India and traveling on the ocean—it was called "crossing the black water," the *kali pana*—was for-

These eight images show the new sugar workers whom the British brought to the Caribbean colony of British Guiana from India to replace freed blacks who did not want to stay on the plantations. The British were eager to show the wealth and prosperity of the Indians, and that one even adopted English clothing. The images are not typical in that far more men than women left India to cross the "black water." But it is true that the indentured workers brought their clothing, languages, and beliefs with them, changing the face of the Caribbean. (NATIONAL MARITIME MUSEUM)

bidden. Anyone who made that fateful passage became impure, polluted.

Hindus in India had a very strong sense of their place in their community. Each person was born into a "caste"—a role in society. Just like Europeans in the Age of Honey, a Hindu was expected to do the work of his or her ancestors. But a person who crossed the black water lost all caste; he was stripped of the connections that had defined him and his family for generations. Anyone who left the country could not come back and be respected by his friends, his family, his fellow villagers, unless he went through a special ceremony.

The *arkatis* (recruiters) who were hired by shipping companies were Indians themselves; they knew villagers would not want to cross the water. But they also knew where there were hungry, desperate people. So they fanned out to the countryside and began to look for strong men. Bharath, who was about to leave for Trinidad, later explained how that happened. His version of English is hard to understand, but it is how the Indians began to speak on the islands. "E no tell e I go chinedad you know . . . e no tell e no come back, e no greet mumma fadder again." ("He did not tell me I was going to Trinidad, you know. He didn't tell me I would never come back, or never see my mother and father again.")

Recruits such as Bharath came to a subdepot, where a district officer took down their information—name, village, caste—and then sent them hundreds of miles away, to the embarkation depot in Calcutta. The wait at the depot—a set of buildings surrounded by a high wall near the harbor—was a strange experience: The workers had probably never ventured far from their villages, and suddenly they were living among people who spoke different languages. Instead of living right next to people whose ancestors knew your ancestors, you were thrown in with people about whom you knew nothing. All were given vaccinations, metal feeding bowls, and warm clothes. The women received jackets, skirts, and petticoats, the men wool trousers and wool jackets and caps and shoes. They agreed to a five-year contract, during which they were to be paid a daily wage, and were given promise of a return passage back to India.

On the day the coolies were to depart, each one was given a "tin ticket," an identification disk, hung around the neck or strapped to the arm. The enslaved Africans who were taken to the sugar plantations lost their names; they were meant to be pure property. The Indian indentures were lied to, they were tricked, they were no more than cheap labor to keep the plantations running—but they were still individuals. Each of their names was carefully recorded in account books.

And then they set off, across the seas.

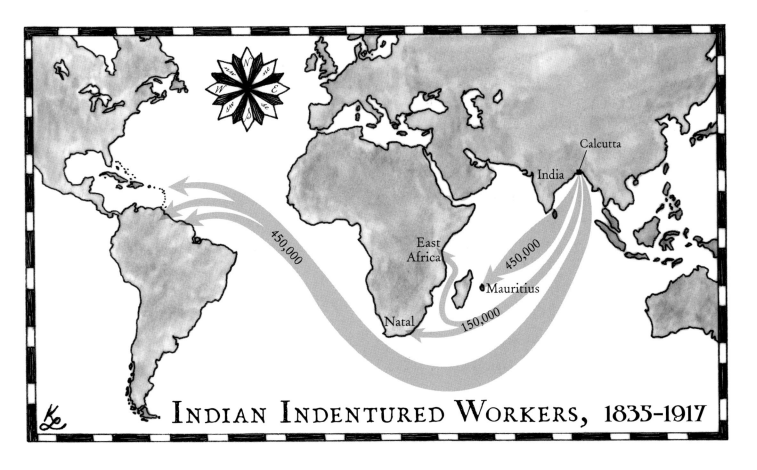

INDIAN INDENTURED WORKERS, 1835–1917

The journey was long—sometimes it lasted for twenty-seven weeks, far longer than the Middle Passage, the journey that brought newly enslaved Africans to the New World. Everyone lived below the deck—men on one side, women and children on the other. They roused early and were allowed on the deck for air, dancing, and singing. But homesickness would often strike them, spreading like a terrible fever; some wasted away out of sadness.

On the ships, something else began to form: a new sense of family. So far away from home, the emigrants called themselves *jahajii-bhai*—ship brothers. This song tells of the hopes the Indians brought with them on the ships:

> *SHIP BROTHERS*
> *Listen my dear, listen*
> *Come along with me*
> *I will get you a good job*
> *Will make you meth [rich], sardar [boss], sahib [master]*
> *Come, I am taking you to a country named Sitiram*
> *This country is by the side of Calcutta*
> *There are mines of gold*
> *There you will get food in utensils of gold*

Together, these ship brothers ventured into the unknown.

## Slavery or Freedom? The In-Between

Indenture was not exactly slavery, but it was not exactly freedom, either. When the new workers, exhausted and disoriented from their trip, arrived in the Caribbean, not much had changed since the days of slavery. At the immigrant depot they were now assigned to a plantation. Then they were taken to the old slave barracks—low shacks where several men shared a small space, slept on wooden cots, and coped with bad drainage and damp floors.

As ever, sugar work was brutally hard. The workers woke early, and for the first few months they were "seasoned"—learning the numbing work of hoeing or weeding or loading the barges with cut cane. After they were broken in, they might take on other tasks or, if they were lucky, get a place at the factory. The Indians' contracts called for seven hours' work for about twenty-four cents a day. During the first few months, though, eight cents a week was deducted for food rations. And no matter what the words said on a piece of paper, sugar workers did not work just seven hours. More often than not, they labored as long as there was light, in the broiling heat. And though they might not be shackled or whipped like slaves, their lives were completely controlled by the terrifying overseers.

Workers could not leave the plantation unless they had a pass. And if they did decide to explore on their own, without permission, they could be thrown in jail, sentenced to hard labor, or lose some of their hard-earned wages. A charge of "idling" in the fields could result in the loss of a whole week's wages. Worse, if they dared rebel or protest, their contract could be transferred to another estate. And there were still complaints of flogging or mysterious deaths. Life, as the historian Hugh Tinker noted, was like being a prisoner on parole.

In the sugar colonies, the wounds of slavery were never far beneath the surface. The Africans who had worked in sugar quickly left the plantations and tried to farm or moved to nearby towns. As one planter said, it made no sense to believe that "the Negro would become a grateful and cheerful free laborer on the soil which had been watered by his tears in slavery." But what could the former slaves do? Every Indian who accepted the paltry wages specified in the indenture contract lowered the price an African could charge for his labor.

The Indian coolies and the ex-slaves, who resented these newcomers flooding into the colonies and driving down wages, were instant rivals. This was convenient for the planters—who were skilled at the game of divide and rule. The planters lumped their workers into two distinct but equally nasty stereotypes: Former slaves were described as lazy, whereas Indians were called meek, docile children. "You may have work and plenty of it for a black man and a coloured man, and they will not do it," claimed planter W. Alleyne Ireland. He conveniently ignored the fact that the ex-slaves wanted to work their own land, not labor for their former owners. The overseers praised the Indians' meekness but also held them in contempt. The Indian, one overseer claimed, "possesses the low, cringing and abject habit common to his nationality."

And yet, for all the hardships and prejudice, most Indians decided to stay in the colonies even after their contracts ended. By the end of the 1800s, only a quarter of the indentures sailed back to India after their five years were over. Sometimes this was because they were still too poor. Others told tales of returning only to be spurned by their villages for having broken caste or to be preyed upon by relatives who stole their money. Most of those who stayed in the New World, though, chose to do so because it offered a new life. And in the late 1800s, the authorities began to make a new offer to Indian workers. If they remained in the Caribbean, they could get a small plot of land of their own. After putting in their time in sugar, they could begin to farm for themselves.

Marina's own family prospered during this time. Her great-grandfather served as a headman on one of the largest plantations in British Guiana, Port Mourant. The land was drier than elsewhere—making people less prone to malaria—and it was here, on the unused green fields, that some of the best cricket was played. A bustling town, also called Port Mourant, sprang up, with schools, even a hospital. Her great-grandmother ran a grocery store, and so they were able to put aside some money and marry one of their daughters to the first Indian lawyer in the colony. Her own grandmother was given a large house as her dowry—the very house Marina later learned had been replaced by an auto repair shop.

By the turn of the twentieth century, the colonies were changing. Sugar still dominated the local economy. But now there were more and more "free" workers—those who had moved off the estates and lived in their own houses, splitting their time between sugar work and their own businesses. There were Indian shopkeepers, traders, and rice growers. The Africans, too, had migrated to the cities, where they became clerks, teachers, or servants in wealthy households. A new society was emerging—one that had its roots in the dark history of slavery but was also moving into the future.

The planters regarded themselves as benevolent rulers of these changing sugar lands, with the coolies as their ignorant and childlike wards. Rulers they were, and they often used the courts to maintain control, not to administer justice. Still, there was a distinct difference from the days of slavery. Now there were laws on the books, not debates about abolition; there were contracts signed by both parties, not just the rule of guns and torture. And we can hear that shift in the voice of one remarkable, mysterious Indian.

# Reform

In 1896, an indentured worker in British Guiana who called himself Bechu began publishing a series of letters to the local newspaper, revealing the conditions on the sugar plantations—or "estates," as they were called. Born in Calcutta, Bechu was an orphan, which put him at the very bottom of society. But he was adopted by a missionary who taught him English, and then he worked for various English people in Calcutta before signing up for his indenture and traveling across the ocean. Bechu made good use of his knowledge of English by writing to the elite newspapers in British Guiana. He exposed one of the tricks the planters used to get around the terms of the indenture contract.

Indians were supposed to work seven hours each day, and to be paid a set fee for each day's work. But the planters instead preferred to pay by the "task"—they insisted that they wouldn't pay a worker until he had completed a specific job. Of course the owner would pick a job that took much more than seven hours, so a worker's day stretched from sunup to sundown. Bechu showed that this was illegal and unfair: "There are lots of indentured men who work by time and have drivers at their backs all day long." Yet, even then, they "do not earn" the amount specified in their contracts.

Several planters wrote back to the paper, furious at the suggestion that they were cheating the coolies. The letters were black with rage—at the Indian who dared to speak up and question the ethics of Englishmen. When a commission was convened in 1897 to investigate the conditions on the estates, Bechu—the Indian the planters hated—came before the judges to share his evidence. This was galling, since some had even questioned whether Bechu, who wrote in such polished English, really was an Indian. But there was more to the planters' outrage than a desire to silence one outspoken Indian.

Underneath the clash over rights, laws, and work rules, there was a deeper truth that the planters were sensing: The Age of Sugar was ending. On the one hand, the work on the plantations was now guided by a web of laws and rules that even an Indian coolie like Bechu could use to challenge the owners. Workers were individuals, not property. On the other hand, world sugar prices were plummeting. Owners no longer had the economic clout of being a mainstay of the economy. Instead, smaller plantations were going bankrupt. The old ways were simply not working anymore. Why were sugar prices falling? Because of competition from another part of the world.

And this is how the stories of Marina's family and Marc's aunt's family finally crossed.

## SUGAR AND SCIENCE

Remember Napoleon's dream of a French sugar empire and how the victorious Haitians destroyed it? The French emperor's grand plan failed, but he was resourceful. If he could not grow and process sugar in the Caribbean, he needed another source. And this was particularly difficult because England's navy was the best in the world. Even if Napoleon could find a place to grow cane, he could not get it past the English ships.

Napoleon was seemingly in an impossible bind, but he found a way out of the sugar trap. Actually the solution already existed—he just needed to hear about it. In 1747, Andraeas Marggraf, a German scientist, cut up and dried some parsnips, then mashed them into a powder.

He did the same with beets. He then carefully extracted the chemical elements that made the powders sweet. These were, he proved, identical to the sugar obtained from cane.

Beets do not need a tropical climate—they grow happily underground even in northern Europe. For the first time in history, a taste native to the tropics was exactly matched by a plant grown in a colder area. It was as if some scientist today discovered that he could get a potato to produce a substance that tasted just like chocolate. Beet sugar was a triumph of reason, of science, over the gifts of nature.

When Napoleon was calculating how to get sugar without having to fight the English fleet, a couple of beet-sugar factories had begun operating around Europe. Napoleon was thrilled, and he ordered the French to begin planting thousands of acres of beets. By 1814, there were more than three hundred factories in France alone, turning beets into sugar.

In 1806 he had come up with a plan: Let the English rule the seas; he, Napoleon, would insist that no country in Europe would buy from them. He would shut them out. Goods from around the world would pile up on English docks, while the people of Europe spent their money on products they'd sell to one another. Unfortunately for Napoleon, his plan to exclude English products failed. Too many Europeans ignored his rules and smuggled in English goods. But the beet-sugar breakthrough did have one important effect in another part of Europe: the Ukraine of Marc's family.

## Serfs and Sweetness

In the 1800s, the Russian czars controlled the largest empire in the world, and yet their land was caught in a kind of time warp. While the

# The Sugar Genius

Refining cane syrup in one boiling vat after another was not only dangerous; it was terribly inefficient. The man who figured out a safe, reliable way to accomplish the same thing with far less labor was himself a product of a slave society. Norbert Rillieux was born in New Orleans in 1806. His father was a wealthy white planter and engineer who recognized that the boy whom he had fathered with a free woman of color was unusually smart. So Norbert's father sent him to France to be educated. There, he learned the same rational, scientific approach to testing and experimenting that had proven that the sugar that comes from beets is the same as that which comes from cane. And when he returned home to Louisiana, he applied his knowledge of engineering to refining sugar. Rillieux figured out that if the sugar syrup was heated in a series of special sealed pans, instead of in open cauldrons, the whole process would be transformed. One person, instead of a team, could oversee the operation, and far less heat would be needed, since the heat could be transferred from one pan to another. Rillieux first demonstrated his invention in the 1840s, and planters were quick to see its value. But even being a noted inventor who had been given his legal freedom by his father was no guarantee of safety to a black man in Louisiana, so he returned to France. Though he was not in danger of being enslaved in France, he suffered through a series of conflicts with others who claimed they had invented his process. Frustrated, he turned his sharp mind to other tasks, such as the study of ancient Egyptian hieroglyphics. Rillieux, who died in Paris in 1894, is a perfect example of the changing world of sugar in the 1800s. He had grown up amidst slavery yet made his reputation by using science. He himself was free but had to struggle against prejudice throughout his life.

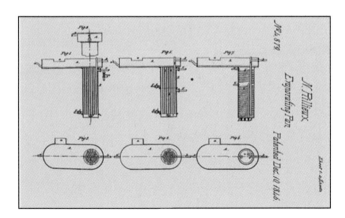

Rillieux's innovative design for a vacuum pan. In the old boiling house, heat escaped; now it is captured and used.

English were building factories, drinking tea, and organizing against the slave trade, the vast majority of Russians were serfs. Serfs were in a position very similar to slaves'—they could not choose where to live, they could not choose their work, and the person who owned their land and labor was free to punish and abuse them as he saw fit. In Russia, serfdom only finally ended in 1861, two years before Abraham Lincoln's Emancipation Proclamation.

Not only were Russian farms run on unfree labor, but they used very simple, old-fashioned methods of farming. Like the English back in the time of Henry III, all Russians aside from the very wealthy still lived in the Age of Honey—sugar was a luxury taken out only when special guests came to visit. Indeed, as late as 1894, when the average English person was eating close to ninety pounds of sugar a year, the average Russian used just eight pounds.

In one part of Russia, though, the nobles who owned the land were interested in trying out new tools, new equipment, and new ideas about how to improve the soil. This area was in the northern Ukraine just crossing into the Russian regions of Voronigh and Hurst. When word of the breakthrough in making sugar reached the landowners in that one more advanced part of Russia, they knew just what to do: plant beets.

Cane sugar had brought millions of Africans into slavery, then helped foster the movement to abolish the slave trade. In Cuba large-scale sugar planting began in the 1800s, brought by new owners interested in using modern technology. Some of these planters led the way in freeing Cuban slaves. Now beet sugar set an example of modern farming that helped convince Russian nobles that it was time to free their millions of serfs. And that is precisely where Marc's family story begins—with

Nina's grandfather, the serf who bought his freedom from figuring out how to color beet sugar.

In the 1890s, the price of cane sugar was declining, and the planters who owned sugar fields in British Guiana were on the edge of bankruptcy. Cane sugar production in Cuba was booming, driving down prices. And beet sugar colored by new processes was now outselling cane sugar from the Caribbean. Nina's Russian grandfather on the Volga and Marina's Indian great-grandfather in Guyana were linked by sugar.

No one could have seen it at the time, but the invention of beet sugar was not just a challenge to cane. It was a hint—just a glimpse, like a twist that comes about two thirds of the way through a movie—that the end of the Age of Sugar was in sight. For beet sugar showed that in order to create that perfect sweetness you did not need slaves, you did not need plantations, in fact you did not even need cane. Beet sugar was a foreshadowing of what we have today: the Age of Science, in which sweetness is a product of chemistry, not whips.

In 1854 only 11 percent of world sugar production came from beets. By 1899 the percentage had risen to about 65 percent. And beet sugar was just the first challenge to cane. By 1879 chemists discovered saccharine—a laboratory-created substance that is several hundred times sweeter than natural sugar. Today the sweeteners used in the foods you eat may come from corn (high-fructose corn syrup), from fruit (fructose), or directly from the lab (for example, aspartame, invented in 1965, or sucralose—Splenda—created in 1976). Brazil is the land that imported more Africans than any other to work on sugar plantations, and in Brazil the soil is still perfect for sugar. Cane grows in Brazil today, but not always for sugar. Instead, cane is often used to create ethanol, much as corn farmers in America now convert their harvest into fuel.

We all crave sweetness, now more than ever since there are so many ways to satisfy that need. And there are still sugar plantations where the work is brutal. In places like the Dominican Republic (Haiti's island neighbor), some sugar work is not very different from what it was for Marina's Indian ancestors in British Guiana: hard, poorly paid labor by people who are often mistreated. But for most of us, chemists have more to say about how we satisfy that taste than do overseers. When sugar is in the headlines, critics speak about how much of it we eat, not who picked the crop. Doctors warn that young people are gaining too much weight from eating sugary snacks; parents learn that kids who drink too many sweet sodas can cycle between manic sugar "highs" and grinding sugar "crashes." No one worries about where the sweetness comes from. Our diet was transformed by the Age of Sugar, but that era is over. And we know just where and when the end finally came: in South Africa, where an Indian lawyer was making a name for himself.

# The Lawyer

Mohandas K. Gandhi (later known as the Mahatma or Great One) was born in India to a traditional Hindu family. When he was given the opportunity to study law in England, he faced the same problem as the indentured sugar workers: He would lose caste if he crossed the black water. His family arranged a special ceremony that allowed him to make the trip without giving up his place in society. Thus, in 1894, freshly educated in England, Gandhi made a second journey. He began practicing law in Natal, a region in what is now South Africa. He moved there because many Indians were already in Natal, laboring as indentured sugar workers.

(left) The cane planters of the Caribbean understood that beets were a real threat, as this typical article from the *Argosy* in what is now Guyana shows.

(top right) This picture of a sugar beet, harvested in Colorado and about to be trimmed, was taken in 1939. During World War II, which America entered two years later, Americans at home were allowed only limited rations of sugar. (LIBRARY OF CONGRESS)

(bottom right) Harvesting sugar beets was not as deadly as cutting sugar cane, but it was difficult work for little pay. This 1915 photo taken by the reformer Lewis Hine shows children ranging in age from ten to eighteen working in the beet sugar fields in Sugar City, Colorado. (LIBRARY OF CONGRESS)

One day, Gandhi later explained, "a man in tattered clothes, headgear in hand, two front teeth broken and his mouth bleeding, stood before me trembling and weeping." The indentured worker, whose name was Balasumdaram, had been badly beaten by his employer. Gandhi knew that Balasumdaram was trapped. For no matter how poorly he had been treated by his boss, if he left the plantation, he could be prosecuted and jailed. Gandhi saw indenture for what it was: "almost as bad as slavery. Like the slave the indentured labourer was the property of his master."

As in British Guiana, Trinidad, and Mauritius, Indians were first brought to Natal to cut cane. Over time, some stayed on to become farmers, clerks, or shopkeepers. They were starting to build their own new community. While the white settlers in Natal were happy to have cheap Indian labor, they were dead set against allowing Indians to live there as equals. So they did everything they could to discourage the Indians—indentured workers were beaten by their employers, arrested, kept to certain areas, or separated from their families. There was no doubt in Gandhi's mind: Indenture *was* a form of slavery.

Even as Gandhi was working for Balasumdaram, the South Africans passed a new law designed to make life difficult for Indians. If an indentured worker chose to stay past his or her contract and settle, the worker was slapped with an annual tax, which was a heavy burden for Indians, who barely survived on their wages. The message was clear: You were brought to Natal only as a guest worker; you have no right to stay. Today in the United States we allow Mexicans and people from Central America to milk cows and to pick tomatoes, strawberries, grapes, and other crops, but Congress has been deadlocked over the rules for allowing them to become residents or citizens. Just like the whites in Natal, we want the cheap labor but are reluctant to offer those same workers and their children a home in our country.

The Indian community in Natal understood the message the whites were sending: Work here, don't stay here. But the Indians were not property; they were not defined by their years of labor as indentures. They wished to be seen as individuals, full and equal citizens who could not be told to leave or treated as second-class members of society. Gandhi traveled back to India, where he spoke to the English government officers who were responsible for Indians in Natal. In the age of the telegraph, news of his words moved swiftly back to South Africa, enraging its white inhabitants. By the time he returned by ship at Christmastime, an angry mob was waiting at the docks, and they surged around Gandhi, throwing rocks and eggs, until Mrs. Alexander, the local police magistrate's wife, fended off the attackers with her parasol. Gandhi was taken to the police station, where he was whisked through a side door disguised in a police uniform.

So far, Gandhi was being a lawyer, an advocate, pleading with whites to offer better treatment for Indians. His message was about to change.

## SATYAGRAHA

Sugar has left a bloody trail through human history. Sugar plantations from Africa to the Caribbean and Louisiana and as far as Hawaii are haunted by stories of brutality, torture, rape, and murder. When slaves rebelled, they often took gruesome revenge on their masters, only to face even more horrific reprisals when the owners and overseers regained control. Indenture was a step better than slavery, but masters did their best to intimidate workers to keep wages low and silence critics. Violence was the very soil from which sugar sprang. The only way to fight sugar masters, it seemed, was for the workers to be harder, tougher, and more willing to accept bloodshed than the owners.

Gandhi began to see that there was a way for the indentured Indians to strengthen themselves without having to rely on machetes and guns. Freedom, he realized, did not come only from rising up against oppressors or tyrants. It could also be found in oneself. The mere fact that the sugar masters treated their workers as some form of property did not mean the Indians had to accept that definition. In fact, it was up to them to claim, to assert, their own worth, their own value. A man who had his inner, personal dignity was free—no matter how a boss tried to bully him. Gandhi's years in South Africa became a laboratory, as he experimented with how to be a truthful, free person. Finally, he was ready to put his ideas into practice.

On September 11, 1906, the Empire Theater in Johannesburg, South Africa, was crowded with Indian delegates, waiting to hear word about the Black Act. The law was due to take effect the next year, and it required every Indian—man, woman, and child over the age of eight—to register and be fingerprinted. Any Indian who did not have proper registration papers could be fined, jailed, or deported. To the Indian community, the registration card was a humiliating symbol of discrimination. They were being treated not just as outsiders, but as potential criminals. Gandhi sat on the stage awaiting his turn to speak. When he stepped up, he looked into the audience and felt he could "read in every face the expectation of something strange to be done or to happen."

Then Gandhi invited each person in the theater to join him in an exceptional oath, a pledge not to register, not to accept the government's rules, even if that resulted in severe punishment. Gandhi insisted that every person weigh the commitment and make a personal choice. "Every individual," he explained, must make the oath him- or herself,

> *facing not to his neighbor, but his God. Nor should it be taken in order to gain power over anybody but oneself, for the power of an oath is defined by what one man can promise to do, and what he is willing to suffer: insult, incarceration, hard labor, flogging, fine, deportation, and even death.*

Everyone in the audience raised his or her hand.

Gandhi bound the crowd together to follow a new path, which he called Satyagraha—which means "truth with force," or "firmness." It is also called "love-force." While the goal of violence is to defeat and vanquish the enemy, the goal of Satyagraha is to convince or convert the opponent. "He must be weaned from error by patience and sympathy." A person who believes in Satyagraha will not fight physically, but instead resists through his or her own inner courage, knowing he might be jailed or beaten.

Passive resistance was not new. Gandhi had read Henry David Thoreau, who advocated exactly this view. But never before had nonviolence been employed for a mass movement. This was a remarkable turning point: Gandhi escaped the cycle of violence breeding violence; he challenged poor workers to show wealthy masters that there is a better way.

Satyagraha is the opposite of the idea that a human being can be made into property by someone else's laws, or guns, or prejudice. Any person can pledge to live up to his highest standards. Then the effort to make good on that vow is what defines us as human beings. We are the sum of our own soul strength, not of the judgments imposed on us by others.

On August 16, 1908, thousands of Indians assembled at Hamida Mosque in Johannesburg Park. The protesters had issued an ultimatum, demanding that the government repeal the Black Act. Then a volunteer came riding up by bicycle with news: The government would not budge. The Black Act would remain in force.

A fire was lit in a giant iron cauldron, and the certificates of 2,300 Indians were tossed into the flames—the first major act of Satyagraha. "I am not property," the Indians were showing. "I am not your victim," they were demonstrating; "I have the power of my conscience," they were proving. The quiet strength of the Indian community shook the South African government. And by June 1914 it gave in; the Black Act was taken off the books. The Indians had insisted that they were not mere workers but were citizens—and finally the government could not resist.

His work done, Gandhi returned to India, where Satyagraha became the most effective weapon in the fight for Indian independence. In India, Gandhi also preached noncooperation—refusing to use or buy British goods. Just as the British abolitionists shamed people into not buying the blood-soaked crystals forged in slavery, he told Indians not to buy goods manufactured by their colonial master. Gandhi's love-force won. In 1947, India became the first British colony since the United States to break free from foreign rule. As we all know, nonviolence and passive resistance would eventually spread through the world, inspiring Martin Luther King, Jr., in the fight for civil rights in America.

The origins of Satyagraha—one of the most revolutionary and potent ideas in recent memory—lay in the moment when Gandhi met the abused indentured man Balasumdaram and when sugar workers, who had been brought around the world to cut cane, rose up to demand their rightful place.

Sugar turned human beings into property, yet sugar led people to reject the idea that any person could be owned by another. Sugar murdered millions, and yet it gave the voiceless a way to speak. Sugar crushed people, and yet it was because of sugar that Gandhi began his experiment in truth—so that every individual could free him- or herself. Only sugar—the sweetness we all crave—could drive people to be so cruel, and to combat all forms of cruelty. The craving for sugar took us from that ancient time when people were defined by the work of their ancestors to our modern world—the one Gandhi led us to see, in which each individual is valued as human. Though terrible conditions for sugar workers still exist in places such as the Dominican

In many parts of the world, sugar is now harvested by machines, its long history fading into the mists. (BRET DUKE, THE TIMES-PICAYUNE)

Republic, and cane sugar has been replaced by other sweeteners invented in the Age of Science, this one substance forever marked our history.

Every day, we live in the world sugar created—where the descendants of Africans live in the Caribbean, in Brazil, in the United States and Canada; where the grandchildren of indentured Indians share those Caribbean islands and American cities; where the children of China, Japan, the Philippines, and Korea make up the population of Hawaii; where Haitians still suffer from the silence that greeted their nation's birth; where equality does not belong to the rich, the planter, the overseer, or even the freed people. It exists in each one of us. That is the sweet truth bought at the price of so much bitter pain.

Sugar changed the world.

# How We Researched and Wrote This Book

*A Short Essay on a (Very) Long Process, for Teachers,*
*Librarians, and Other Interested Parties*

*Note: This essay is not aimed at young readers, but rather at those who challenge, instruct, and assist them. It is based on the firm conviction that young people are smart, and therefore the more opportunity we give them to think about big questions in creative ways, the better. Here we outline the really large historical themes that came up in our research. Our book is not a textbook, so we could not pause to spell out and debate these questions. Instead, we trust that creative teachers will use what we have written in the main text, and the suggested sources we point out here, as a starting point and will go on to explore further in their classes. We also use this essay to outline some of the research and writing strategies we used, which may be a useful model for students.*

*Any adult who thinks the kinds of questions we discuss in this essay are beyond the ken of middle and high school students need only read some of the National History Day prize essays written by students as young as seventh-graders—available at www.historycooperative. org/journals/ht/40.1.dabel.html—or those written by high school students and published in the Concord Review, www.tcr.org/tcr/index.htm. The more intellectual stimulation we offer to young people, the higher they rise.*

When we began reading about sugar, we soon realized that the story of that one product pointed directly at two key historical questions. First: How were sugar and slavery related to the struggle for freedom? This involves the American, French, and Haitian revolutions and the abolitionist movements in those countries as well as in England. Second: How were sugar and slavery entangled with the birth of the Industrial Revolution in England? As you will see in the notes, historians have been debating these questions for decades. Yet all too often students, especially in high school, are presented with completely separate units on, say, slavery in the United States; the Enlightenment and the Declaration of Independence; the French Revolution; the Industrial Revolution in England; and abolitionism and the Civil War—as if these crucial historical themes were not inextricably linked. If our book accomplishes nothing more than to encourage teachers to teach slavery in North America as a small part of a much larger system primarily focused on the Caribbean and Brazil—with all that implies for understanding slavery, African American history, race, and the United States as part of a larger world—we will have succeeded.

How does a clear look at sugar and slavery change how we see ideas of freedom and the invention of new kinds of work and machinery? Speaking in very broad terms, the academic debate goes like this: The story of sugar is grim and brutal. The more they get to know that dark history, the more some historians distrust the ideas of freedom and liberty expressed by planters who owned slaves, and the more they see the Industrial Revolution as a product of whips and chains, not inventions and science. They see the tortured slaves and the planters' profits as exposing the lies of the time. The drive to abolish slavery itself is seen as serving the "interests" of a new class of wealthy men. Other historians believe that even people who profited from sugar and slaves could have had their consciences stirred, or see industrialization as more a product of new machines than of profits from plantations. Researching slavery forces each of us to decide whether to view the past through the eyes of the skeptic or the idealist. These are fascinating issues that go to the heart of how we see the birth of the modern age, and we believe they suggest perfect questions to pose to bright students.

Teachers will know the best ways to frame these issues for their own students. But the basic outline is clear: When we discuss slavery and ideals of equality in American History the discussion quickly becomes personal—were the slaveholding Founding Fathers hypocrites? But the interplay of glorious principles and brutal enslavement looks different when we consider the real scope of sugar slavery and the full breadth of the age of political and industrial revolutions. Instead of speaking about individuals, we are trying to understand the deepest, most basic drives of human behavior: Are we driven by greed? By our economic system? By our ideals? By technological change? By something as vague and hard to define as the spirit of an age? Who are we? What makes us able to be so inhumane? What enables us to break those chains and act on our common humanity? No historical questioning could be more rewarding for students and teachers alike.

Researching and writing this book took far more time than we (and Virginia Buckley, our editor, who showed the patience of a saint) imagined. As we discovered, writing about sugar required two large-scale, and opposing, efforts. First we had to cast an ever-widening net.

The subjects discussed in this book took place over thousands of years and in almost every habitable corner of this planet—so how did we research them? Our strategy was to begin with books that had already done the basic spadework. After reading those so-called secondary works (the books are about sugar; they are not the actual documents, the "primary sources" of sugar history), we were ready to turn to more specialized studies. We wanted to feature the lives of sugar workers whenever possible, and searching for those voices took us to transcripts of interviews and other archival materials. But we didn't look for those voices until we understood where they fit into the larger narrative. Most students given a research topic will head straight for a search engine. But we didn't. To begin with, we read books that gave us a basic sense of the story; then we used the Internet to explore further. That is not because of a distrust of the Internet, but, rather, because a search engine yields such a random collection of sites—we saw no reason to begin by being overwhelmed and confused. We wanted the Internet to be a tool guided by our knowledge and interests, not a flood of stuff we needed to sort through. But understanding these big issues was only half our challenge.

Our second task was compression—finding a way to write about this vast story that was neither a litany of facts nor an endless tome. We kept revising and revising to get to the essence of the story, while whenever possible featuring human beings, not just economic, political, and social forces.

Having two authors, two sets of eyes, four hands, helped. Marc did most of the basic research and roughed out the manuscript. Marina used her novelist's eye to edit and focus that draft text, and then tapped her own research and scholarship on Indians and indenture. Then we both revised again to make sure our styles blended well and the book added up to a coherent whole.

We owe a great debt to Dr. Rachel Mattson and Dr. Terri Ruyter, creators of the Becoming Historians website, www.becominghistorians.org, and directors of a Teaching America project through the New York University Department of Teaching and Learning. Through Rachel and Terri, and for two consecutive summers, we were able to present our work in progress to New York City elementary school teachers (the first summer K–5, the second all fifth-grade instructors). Working with them was invaluable to us, as it helped us to find the core of our story and taught us how best to connect with both students and the adults who work with them. That summer work was our field test.

While students in class will not have the benefit of a cowriter, or a room full of eager listeners, they can follow the same general arc we did: Go wide to follow every lead and gather too much, then narrow down to find the individuals, the stories, and the themes that communicate most directly to readers.

From the first we envisioned this as a book in which pictures would be as important as words. We owe an immense debt of gratitude to the brilliant designer Trish Parcell for making that vision a reality, to Renee Cafiero for her painstaking eye, and to the entire team at Clarion and in Boston, including Kerry Martin, Daniel Nayeri, and Christine Kettner, for sharing our passion to make each page perfect.

# Acknowledgments

We were immensely fortunate that very early in our research, we had the chance to meet with the scholar whose book is the first reference all serious students of sugar in history must read. Dr. Sidney Mintz published *Sweetness and Power* (hereafter SP; bibliographic information on all materials mentioned here and in the Notes can be found in the Bibliography on page 155) in 1985, and everyone since then has used it as a touchstone. Mintz is an anthropologist by training, and he captured not only the facts of sugar history but how sugar transformed the lives of those who grew it, sold it, and ate it.

Sugar plantations stand between the old agricultural world of the feudal period and the wage and factory labor of the industrial age. Any historian who links social change to shifts in economic systems must account for them. Mintz led the way in doing this—and in a most insightful, probing, and convincing book.

In that same initial trip, we also got to know Dr. Franklin Odo, program director of the Asian Pacific American Program at the Smithsonian Institution. Dr. Odo is an authority on the history of Hawaii, and thus on that part of the sugar story. Not only did he help guide us at the start, but he reviewed the entire manuscript at the end, and we were greatly helped by his insights. As we neared the conclusion of our work, we read *Out of the East* (hereafter OE) by Dr. Paul Freedman and found it both immensely helpful and fun to read. Dr. Freedman and his Yale graduate students Adam Franklin-Lyons and Azelina Jaboulet-Vercherre took time to answer our questions, and Dr. Freedman reviewed the entire book and gave us the benefit of his fine historical judgment. Our thanks, too, to special collections librarians Christina Riquelmy at Louisiana State University and Erich Kesse at Florida State University, who helped us find archival materials, and to professor Rick Halpern, of New College in Toronto, for insights on sugar in both Louisiana and South Africa. Dr. Nurhan Atasoy and the Turkish Cultural Mission in Washington, D.C., were especially helpful in researching images of sugar sculpture in the Ottoman period. We were grateful to Dr. Douglas Herman for directing us to Professor David Burney, who sent us a paper he coauthored that uses charcoal found in nine locations on the island of Kaua'i to date human arrival in the Hawaiian Islands. Professor Ben Lapidus was a most helpful guide to the music that came out of sugar slavery.

Needless to say, while we are grateful for all the insights from these scholars, this is our book, and everything in it—or left out of it—is a product of our decisions. We are aware of two books aimed at adults that, like ours, use sugar as a pathway through world history: Peter Macinnis, *Bittersweet* (hereafter B); and Elizabeth Abbott, *Sugar: A Bittersweet History* (hereafter SBH). We found Macinnis a useful source for dates and stories, but somewhat scattered and frustrating to read. We learned of Abbott's research from Dr. Halpern but did not actually see her book until ours was written. Teachers, parents, and serious students who want to know more about the subjects we cover will find much to consider in Abbott's book.

Marina began her research into the history of indenture with the study that first really investigated this history: *A New System of Slavery: The Export of Indian Labour Overseas, 1830–1920* by Hugh Tinker. Since then, a number of other scholars have fleshed out the story, and even disputed the idea that indenture was another form of slavery. Some scholars whose works feature this newer view include Walton Look Lai in *Indentured Labor, Caribbean Sugar: Chinese and Indian Migrants to the West Indies, 1838–1918* (Baltimore: Johns Hopkins University Press, 1995); Basdeo Mangru, *A History of East Indian Resistance on the Guyana Sugar Estates: 1869–1948* (Lewiston, N.Y.: Edwin Mellen Press, 1996); and Marina Carter, who has done a great deal of work around Indian indentured workers in Mauritius, for instance: *Voices from Indenture: Experiences of Indian Migrants in the British Empire* (London: Leicester University Press, 1996).

As a writer, Marina was especially drawn to scholarship that has excavated the lost "voices" of indenture. For the motivated reader and teacher, this is an excellent way to encounter primary documents and hear all the people involved in indenture. These are as follows: *Maharani's Misery: Narratives of a Passage from India to the Caribbean* by Verene A. Shepherd (Kingston, Jamaica: University of the West Indies Press, 2002); Clem Seecharan's *Bechu: Bound Coolie Radical in British Guiana, 1894–1901* (Kingston, Jamaica: University of the West Indies Press, 1999); and Noor Kumar Mahabir's *The Still Cry*. Mohandas K. Gandhi's autobiography, *The Story of My Experiments with Truth*, also gives a glimpse into his work among the Indian community in South Africa.

Mintz, Macinnis, and various Internet sites got us started—they gave us the basic arc of the story we needed to tell. But that was the shallow end. To really understand sugar, and to hear the voices of sugar workers, we had to swim out to the deep water—the academic studies of sugar, slavery, and indenture. Having done that research, we can tell you that, if you find the subjects in this book interesting, there is a wealth of material out there for you to explore. We hope this book does for you what Mintz did for us: provide the grounding that allows you to be intelligently curious.

# TIMELINE

**Master Timeline:** *Sugar in World History*

## B.C.

| | |
|---|---|
| 8000–7000 | First planting of wild sugar cane, on the island of New Guinea |
| 6000 | Sugar cane reaches the Philippines |
| 1500–900 | Sugar cane used in Hindu ceremonies described in oral traditions that date from around this time |
| 515 | According to the Greek author Herodotus, the Persians had found what may be sugar cane in what is now India and Pakistan |
| 327 | Nearchus, friend of Alexander the Great, again mentions the reed that makes honey without bees, in India |
| 286 | First mention of sugar cane in China |

## A.D.

| | |
|---|---|
| 100 | Sugar mill described in an Indian text |
| 500s | College at Jundi Shapur brings together scholars and doctors from many lands; knowledge of how to grow, refine, and use sugar as a medicine shared |
| 600s | Muslims conquer Jundi Shapur, spread knowledge of sugar throughout rapidly expanding Islamic world |
| 600–1100 | Polynesians bring cane to islands across Pacific; plant reaches Hawaii by 1100 |
| 900s on | Sugar plantations established in Muslim Mediterranean and Spain |
| 1095 on | Crusades: Europeans see sugar growing in the Holy Land |
| 1150–1300 | Champagne fairs—Europeans trade with Muslims for sugar |
| 1200s on | Egyptians become masters of refining whitest sugar |

| 1226 | King Henry III of England pays equivalent of $450 for three pounds of sugar |
| 1402 | Spanish begin conquest of Canary Islands |
| 1420s | Portuguese conquer Madeira Islands |
| 1439 | Europeans reach uninhabited Azores Islands |
| 1450 | Island of Madeira is a leading sugar producer for Europe |
| 1493 | Columbus brings a sugar cane plant to Hispaniola |

## England and Sugar

| 1625 | The English capture Barbados |
| 1665 | The English conquer Jamaica |
| 1760 | Tackey's Rebellion, Jamaica |
| 1772 | Somerset case: A British judge's ruling is interpreted to mean that slaves become free on touching English soil (see France 1691); his actual words, though, were much more specific and were not meant to become a general rule |
| 1786 | Thomas Clarkson's prize-winning abolitionist essay is published |
| 1789 | Olaudah Equiano's autobiography is published |
| 1790s | Cause of abolition in England harmed by bloody example of France |
| 1807 | The English make the slave trade illegal |
| 1833 | England abolishes slavery |
| 1840s–1917 | Indenture |

## France, Sugar, Slavery

| 1685 | Code Noir makes slavery legal in the French sugar colonies |
| 1691 | Slaves are granted liberty when they touch soil of France |
| 1697 | France and Spain divide Hispaniola |
| 1700s | Saint Domingue (the French side of Hispaniola) becomes the world's richest sugar colony |
| 1716 | Pauline case reaches the courts |
| 1789 | French Revolution begins with the declaration of the Rights of Man and the Citizen |
| 1791 | Children of free parents in French sugar colonies are granted the full rights of French |

citizens, no matter what their color or origin; slavery abolished within borders of France

| | |
|---|---|
| 1792 | French leaders begin to use the guillotine to execute enemies |
| 1793 | Louis XVI executed; Marie Antoinette executed |
| 1794 | Slavery abolished in all French sugar colonies |
| 1799 | Napoleon takes power in France |
| 1800 | Napoleon gains control of the center of North America—the Louisiana Territory—from Spain, plans to use it to feed and supply his sugar islands |
| 1802 | Napoleon makes slavery legal again |
| 1803 | Seeing that he will lose in Saint Domingue, Napoleon sells Louisiana Territory to Jefferson |
| Early 1800s | Napoleon encourages beet farming and mills to create beet sugar in France |
| 1814 | France has 334 factories making beet sugar |

## Haiti

| | |
|---|---|
| 1493 | Columbus brings first sugar plants to Hispaniola |
| 1779 | "Colored" soldiers from Saint Domingue join the Americans in the siege of Savannah |
| 1791 | Alligator Woods oath |
| 1793 | Slavery abolished in Saint Domingue; British send army there |
| 1798 | British surrender to Toussaint |
| 1801 | Toussaint frees all slaves in Saint Domingue |
| 1802 | French troops led by Napoleon's brother-in-law land in Saint Domingue; Toussaint captured by French |
| 1803 | Toussaint dies in France; French forces in Saint Domingue surrender |
| 1804 | Haiti declares its independence |

## British North America–United States

| | |
|---|---|
| 1733 | Molasses Act places tax on sugar products not from English islands—colonists generally ignore the law |
| 1764 | Sugar Act stiffens enforcement of rules on trade with sugar islands; colonists protest |

against "taxation without representation"

1765    Rhode Island men disguised as Indians roll barrels of molasses off the *Polly* to protest Sugar Act

1773    Boston Tea Party

1798    President John Adams meets with Joseph Bunel, an ally of Toussaint's; this is the first time an American president publicly dines with a person of African descent

1804    President Thomas Jefferson refuses to recognize Haiti

1800s    Sugar masters from Haiti begin to arrive in Louisiana, making Louisiana into a sugar state

1808    United States follows England in making importation of slaves illegal

1835    First sugar plantation in Hawaii

1852    Chinese workers first come to Hawaii

1862    Abraham Lincoln recognizes Haiti

1863    Emancipation Proclamation

1868    Japanese workers arrive in Hawaii

1875    Sugar from Hawaii is allowed into United States with no extra charges

## Age of Science

1747    Andraeas Marggraf discovers that beet sugar is identical to cane sugar

1840s    Beets become a major crop in Ukraine

1852    Indians begin to arrive in Natal to work in sugar

1861    Czar Alexander II frees Russia's serfs

1879    Saccharine, a chemical sweetener, invented

1906    Gandhi leads Indians, many of them sugar workers, in Johannesburg in an oath to resist discriminatory laws by peaceful means

1965    Aspartame, an artificial sweetener, invented

1967    High-fructose corn syrup invented

1976    Sucralose (Splenda) invented

21st century    Brazil using much of its sugar-cane crop to produce ethanol

# WEB GUIDE TO COLOR IMAGES

Many of the images reproduced in black and white in this book can also be found in color on the Web. Here we list links to sites that were active as of the time this book went to press. You can also go to marcaronson.com and, using the labeled tab, find all of these links. These links will probably be most useful for teachers using SMART Boards and for students looking for images for their own reports. A book is one product of a research journey, but there is no reason why it should be the only one.

*p. x* Any Net image search will give many color versions of the botanical drawing, such as plants. usda.gov/java/profile?symbol=SAOF. *Saccharum officinarum.*

*p. 12* For a large full-color image of Durga, including offerings made to the goddess, go to www.hindutempleofmichiana.org/Durga2.jpg.

*p. 14* Firdawsi's poem has been illustrated many ways, and you can see more than six thousand of those images by going to the website of the Shahnama Project: shahnama.caret.cam.ac.uk/shahnama/faces/user/index.

*p. 20* To see the Levni drawing, go to www.e-turchia.com/IMAGES /Calendario_agosto_n._2.jpg.

*p. 25* "Collecting Aloe Wood" is the image in the upper left quarter of the painting seen at www.1st-art-gallery.com/Robinet-Testard/Illustration -From-The-Book-Of-Simple-Medicines-By-Mattheaus-Platearius-D.C .1161-C.1470-44.html.

*p. 42* The William Clark series can be found here, at the British Library in its Caribbean Views online exhibit: www.bl.uk/onlinegallery/onlineex /carviews/p/022zzz0001786c9u00003000.html.

*p. 48* Jack Delano's color slides of sugar workers in Puerto Rico can be found on the Library of Congress site at www.loc.gov. Start with the bibliographic information for these two to see the many others:
Call number: LC-USF35-403 <P&P>[P&P]
Reproduction number: LC-DIG-fsac-1a34013 (digital file from original slide); LC-USF351-403 (color film copy slide)
Call number: LC-USF35-392 <P&P>[P&P]
Reproduction number: LC-DIG-fsac-1a34005 (digital file from original slide); LC-USF351-392 (color film copy slide)

*p. 55* For images of music and dance related to sugar slavery, visit the image library that the University of Virginia created to relate to the Atlantic Slave trade at hitchcock.itc.virginia.edu/Slavery/index.php. Look at the chapter called "Music, Dance and Recreational Activities," though the whole site is related to themes of this book and well worth exploring.

For more images of sugar workers in the Dominican Republic today, view the video trailer at www.thepriceofsugar.com/trailer.shtml.

*p. 60* For the Campe image, go to www.howard.edu/library/Scholarship @Howard/Legacy/7.htm.

*p. 64* You can just see the drawing of the banquet for Queen Christina on the left in this exhibit from the Sugar Museum in San Diego: www.sugarmuseum.org/ottoman.html.

*p. 66* The Collins painting of the family drinking tea can be found at collections.vam.ac.uk/item/O56103/oil-painting-a-family-of-three-at/.

*p. 80* To see the Amelie Opie illustrations in color, go to the British Library online gallery at www.bl.uk/onlinegallery/onlineex/carviewsvirtex/afrtrade/blackmanlam/012zzz000t12712u00017000.html.

# Notes and Sources

## Abbreviations Used in These Notes

ACAS • Sheridan, "Africa and the Caribbean in the Atlantic Slave Trade"
B • Macinnis, *Bittersweet*
BTC • Hochschild, *Bury the Chains*
D • Harms, *The Diligent*
EIC • Wild, *The East India Company*
FCC • Williams, *From Columbus to Castro*
IN • Equiano, *The Interesting Narrative*, in Barksdale and Kinnamon,
*Black Writers of America*
MTD • Burnard, *Mastery, Tyranny, and Desire*
OE • Freedman, *Out of the East*
RFP • Curtin, *The Rise and Fall of the Plantation Complex*
ROM • Banfield, *The Rights of Man, the Reign of Terror*
SAC • Morgan and Morgan, *The Stamp Act Crisis*
SBH • Abbott, *Sugar: A Bittersweet History*
SM • Follett, *The Sugar Masters*
SP • Mintz, *Sweetness and Power*
SS • Sheridan, *Sugar and Slavery*
TB • Schwartz, *Tropical Babylons*
VS • Eltis, "The Volume and Structure of the Transatlantic Slave Trade"

The maps throughout were based on a number of sources, including: Peter Mancinnis' *Bittersweet* (Crows Nest, Australia: Allen & Unwin, 2002, pages 3, 17, 26) and Peter Ashdown's *Caribbean History in Maps* (Longman, Caribbean: Trinidad, 1979, pages 17, 18, 31).

*p. 7* Virgil: This short excerpt can be found on a site about bees and honey: www.bee-hexagon.net/en/creativeexpression.htm; or, if you are interested in Roman poetry and would like to see it in the context of the larger poem, go to www.piney.com/Georgics.IV.html.

*p. 8* The Shoshone chief is quoted in Stephen Ambrose, *Undaunted Courage*, page 281.

*p. 9* The story of Alexander, India, and Nearchus is in every history of sugar; see SP, page 20, where the author questions if that particular reed was sugar cane. To go a step beyond those summaries, we went to "Nearchus Discovers a Sea Route from India to the Arabian Peninsula" (www.bookrags.com/research/nearchus-discovers-a-sea-route-from-scit-011/), which is readable, short, and informative. We then learned that Nearchus was actually quoted in a book by the Roman geographer Strabo, who straddled the first century B.C. and the first century A.D. (three hundred years after Nearchus). For Strabo (himself quoted in Pliny the Elder, whose *Natural History* came out in A.D. 77), see *Greek and Roman Technology* by John W. Humphrey et al., page 165; or go to the useful Ancient History Sourcebook site and look up Strabo, Book XV, *On India, 20:* www.fordham.edu/halsall/ancient/strabo-geog-book15-india.html. Clearly, a simple quotation that can be found in many places actually has a longer and more layered history.

*p. 11* Though scholars are not sure when people first arrived in the Hawaiian Islands, and from a glance at the Internet, it is easy to find dates from A.D. 300 all the way to A.D. 1100, there is an emerging consensus. Professor David Burney sent us his coauthored paper "Charcoal Stratigraphies for Kuai'i and the Timing of Human Arrival," which finds that the physical evidence strongly points toward the later dates, around 1100.

*p. 12* The *Atharva Veda:* Again, this beat in the sugar story is found in every general history of the subject, but we were curious to know more. Our research led us to H. W. Magoun's "The Asuri-Kalpa: A Witchcraft Practice of the Atharva-Veda," an article in the *American Journal of Philology.* This extremely dense and scholarly piece gave us a more specific sense of how sugar was used in rituals. Professor Brian Hatcher, dean at Tufts University and a scholar of various Indian languages, was kind enough to confirm the translations of the two Sanskrit terms for sugar.

*p. 13* Jundi Shapur: This is in every standard history, and while we were especially curious to learn more about this university, we did not have much luck. We found a few articles on sites devoted to Persian history, such as Manouchehr Saadat Noury's First Iranian Academic Site: Jundishapur, www. iranian.com/main/blog/m-saadat-noury/first-iranian-academic-site-jundishapur.

Jundi Shapur is mentioned in many articles, sites, and books on the history of Islamic medicine, such as www.muslimheritage.com/topics/default.cfm?ArticleID=679; and it also comes up in histories of Nestorian Christianity, such as www.everyculture.com/Africa-Middle-East/Nestorians-History-and-Cultural-Relations.html. One website indicated that American and Iranian archaeologists were working on the site, but it is dated 2005 and we could find no later reference to this work. Very likely tensions between the two countries have put the research on hold; see also www.cais-soas.com/News/2005/June2005/12-06-iranian.htm.

Any motivated reader who would like to investigate a place where the cultures of the world met 1,500 years ago is likely to find a rich subject in Jundi Shapur. There is one weird twist to this story. The otherwise often admirable educator and visionary Rudolph Steiner announced that Jundi Shapur, via later incarnations of people involved with it, was a dark influence on humanity. We suspect that, to his credit, he understood that the university was an important meeting place for scholars; but living in the 1920s, he saw the abstract, heartless rationality that had left so many dead in World War I as a dark force, and invented the fantasy that Jundi Shapur was one place where that view took hold. Just one more curious byway you discover as you follow the thread of sugar.

*p. 15* For *sharkara*, see B, pages 5–7. On savory tastes, see OE, pages 12–28.

*p. 17* If you are interested in the history of numbers, try Karl Menninger's *Number Words and Number Symbols*. While the text is written at an adult/college level, it is filled with illustrations and photos that are just fascinating to browse through. For Indian-Arabic numerals and their spread to Europe, see pages 406–45.

*p. 18* For "whitest and purest," and in general sugar in Egypt, see L.A.G. Strong, *The Story of Sugar*, page 59. This is a readable adult history, useful as background. For Marco Polo, see Marco Polo, *The Travels*, page 233.

*p. 21* This page owes a great deal to OE; the author tackles the myth of spices and spoiled meat on page 3.

*p. 21* For the Champagne fairs, see Jean Favier, *Gold and Spices*, pages 26–27, and P. Boissonnade, *Life and Work in Medieval Europe*, pages 171–72. For the Muslim names for fabrics, see Henri Pirenne, *Economic and Social History of Medieval Europe*, page 143; for the spice trade in medieval Europe, see pages 141–43. We found all three books, and more, using Questia, a subscription-based online full-text library. They are older books aimed at adults but offer the kinds of details we would not have found anywhere else. Next to Jundi Shapur, the Champagne fairs were the most interesting unexpected sidelight—and avenue for future exploration—that we discovered in researching this book.

*p. 23* OE quotes Jean de Joieville, the fourteenth-century biographer of France's King Louis IX, on page 89. For the sixteenth-century physician Tabernaemontanus on "Nice white sugar," see Richard Feltoe, *Redpath: The History of a Sugar House*. (The page seems to be 13, but as the book displayed on Google Book, we could not make out page numbers.) SP tells the story of Henry III and his quest for a few pounds of sugar on page 82. On the other hand, maggierose.20megsfree. com/sugar.html, a website that appears to be based on archival research, claims sugar was less rare and expensive than the story of King Henry would suggest.

*p. 24* For this description of the Crusader and sugar, see in Stuart Schwartz, ed., *Tropical Babylons* (hereafter TB), "Sugar in Iberia" by William D. Phillips Jr., pages 31–32. This is a highly academic book with chapters by different scholars. We found it most useful for finding quotations and correcting dated or mistaken views repeated in more general surveys. AP or IB teachers might find it a useful resource to supplement books such as SP, or to locate telling details.

*p. 26* This characteristic of sugar—the need to process each crop quickly—is discussed in all the literature. Some books treat the need to grind the crop quickly as entirely a matter of botany, while others indicate some skepticism about the absolute need for that speed. For a good summary of the economic reasons for moving quickly from harvest to milling and boiling, see Philip Curtin, *The Rise and Fall of the Plantation Complex* (hereafter RFP), pages 4–5. Like SP, this is an essential book on sugar and slavery that any IB or AP teacher or high school student doing independent research on these subjects needs to know. While aimed at a college-level audience, it is clear, well written, and smart, so a motivated high school student should be able to dip into it without much difficulty.

*p. 27* Curtin, RFP, summarizes the ways in which sugar plantations were a new form of farming on pages 10–13.

*p. 29* Sugar was often called "white gold." See TB, "Sugar Islands" by Alberto Vieira, page 65.

*p. 32* For a summary of the spread of sugar planting from one part of the New World to another, see SP, pages 32–39; and RFP, pages 73–85. A great deal of careful scholarly attention has been paid to tracking down the statistics of slavery, and this is an area AP teachers would do well to examine with their students. For the numbers of Africans taken to Brazil, see portal.unesco.org/ci/en/ev. php-URL_ID=8161&URL_DO=DO_TOPIC&URL_SECTION=201.html. The statistics on Brazil are skewed because the slave trade continued through the nineteenth century, after it was abolished by England and the United States. But even taking that into account, more Africans were taken to Brazil than any other place.

*p. 32* SP discusses the universal human liking for sweetness on pages 16–18.

*p. 35* We used the version of *The Interesting Narrative of the Life of Olaudah Equiano, or Gustavus Vassa, the African* (hereafter IN) found in Richard Barksdale and Keneth Kinnamon, eds., *Black Writers of America*, a handy reference book that Marina had from her college days. There is a debate among scholars about whether Equiano was actually born in Africa, as he claimed, or perhaps in South Carolina. That as-yet-inconclusive argument is nicely outlined in Adam Hochschild, *Bury the Chains* (hereafter BTC), a highly readable and well-researched book that we frequently used, and that served as a model for the kind of writing we aimed to emulate; see its appendix, pages 369–72. While Equiano's birthplace remains obscure, his account of life in Caribbean slavery is not in question.

*p. 36* For "we were conducted," see IN, page 21.

*p. 36* Since the sugar cycle was similar in all the New World sugar lands, we ranged among sources, looking for the most vivid descriptions and quotations. Both Richard Sheridan's article "Africa and the Caribbean in the Atlantic Slave Trade" (hereafter ACAS) and SBH use the same images of the sugar cycle in Antigua that we reproduce here. For the count of holes per day, see SBH, page 83. For "their huts," OE, page 26. For yet another well-researched account of the sugar labor, see SBH, pages 80–99. The count of rats in Jamaica appears on page 83. For "the hogmeat gang," see SBH, page 82.

*p. 37* (Trade sidebar) For Beekman and sugar in colonial New York, see Edwin Burrows and Mike Wallace, *Gotham*, pages 118–37.

Marc stumbled on the Indian cloth aspect of the so-called triangle trade while researching this book. *The Diligent* (hereafter D) by Robert Harms uses the diary of a French officer on a 1731 slaving voyage as a way to describe the slave trade. Marc was reading it to look for scenes and stories when, on page 81, he learned that 40 percent of the cargo on that ship taken from France to Africa to purchase slaves was either fabrics from India or cowry shells from the Maldive Islands (near India). Further research into the history of the Indian cloth trade in the 1600s and 1700s revealed that this percentage was typical of ships from other European countries, and that the Indians liked to be paid in silver. In turn, Herbert Klein, an esteemed scholar of the slave trade, points out in TB, page 222, that the supposed America-back-to-Europe leg of the standard triangle trade was the exception, not the rule. European ships sailed directly from the sugar islands back to their home ports, while others finished their voyages in North America, most of the crew staying there, with only the captain and a few crew members finding a ride back across the Atlantic.

*p. 39* For the blessing of the mill, the 1689 report, and, more generally, a description of the full sugar-making cycle in Brazil, see TB, pages 176–80. For a parallel account based on the British islands, see Richard Sheridan, *Sugar and Slavery* (hereafter SS), pages 112–18. The two sections share nearly identical titles, which Schwartz surely did on purpose to echo the famous earlier work, but which also proves our point about the common strands in sugar work on the New World plantations. The article ACAS is actually this same book, *Sugar and Slavery*, as summarized by the author in a magazine for historians. Sheridan was one of the deans of scholarship on sugar and slavery of an earlier generation, and his book is not only informative but highly readable. Teachers or AP students would do well to go to Sheridan before turning to more dense and recent monographs that challenge or update his work.

p. 40 For "the image of Hell," see TB, page 3; for "great open mouths," see page 179.

p. 41 For "boiler," see SS, page 115; for "mothers of the platform," see TB, page 179.

p. 54 We are grateful to Dr. Rachel Mattson for these insights into bomba, based on her own research and discussions with dancers and drummers. A glance at YouTube will allow curious readers to see and hear bomba and Maculelê. We also used the bomba entry at the National Geographic World Music site worldmusic.nationalgeographic.com/view/page.basic/genre/content.genre/bomba_696/en_US.

p. 54 Professor Ben Lapidus told us about the rumba link to slavery and supplied the words for the quoted song.

p. 56 (Maroon sidebar): On Palmares, see www.brazil-brasil.com/cvroct95.htm. This is a readable and informative article from a magazine about Brazil; we also used Pedro Paulo Funari et al., *Historical Archaeology*, pages 308–49, which told us how archaeology shades the picture of Palmares that came down from verbal and written accounts. For maroons, we urge teachers and students to explore

"Creativity and Resistance," a website with many resources, developed by the Smithsonian Institution: www.folklife.si.edu/resources/maroon/presentation.htm; Richard Price, a fine scholar of sugar and slavery, has an article within the Teacher's Guide portion of the site that we found particularly helpful: www.folklife.si.edu/resources/maroon/educational_guide/23.htm. Price mentions "cockpit country" and the other inaccessible places in which maroons made their homes.

*p. 57* For Thistlewood, a review article by slavery expert Ira Berlin ("Masters of Their Universe" in *The Nation*, November 2004, available at www.thenation.com/doc/20041129/berlin), compares Thistlewood on page 4 with Landon Carter, a wealthy planter in Virginia who also kept a diary. This is a handy, and insightful, introduction to Thistlewood and, more generally, the position of the overseer on the sugar islands. Berlin is reviewing Trevor Burnard's *Mastery, Tyranny, and Desire* (hereafter MTD), which carefully examines Thistlewood's diary. Any teacher or AP or IB student who wants an unsparing picture of life on the sugar islands in all its brutality should know this book. Douglas Hall's *In Miserable Slavery* is also based on Thistlewood's diary and was a useful resource for us. For the breakdown of the population of Jamaica, see page xxi. For "these overseers," see IN, page 26.

*p. 58* The 1994 film version of *Mansfield Park* chose to make these connections to sugar slavery—which are implied in the novel—visible and central to the plot. While this film can be a wonderful teaching tool, a few of the images are explicit, and teachers will need to see the film first before deciding if it is appropriate to screen in class.

*pp. 58–59* For Thistlewood's experience when he first arrived, see MTD, page 3; for "gagged him," see page 104.

*p. 61* For "nothing is," see IN, page 27.

*p. 61* Acton's quote can be found by copying it into a search engine—it is in every book of famous quotations. Try www.quotationspage.com/quote/27321.html.

*p. 61* For "requires," see IN, page 27. Readers whose understanding of slavery is based on history within the borders of the United States will find this breakdown of the Atlantic slave trade surprising, but it is commonplace for anyone who has even begun reading about the Caribbean and Brazil. For a thorough and recent breakdown of the Atlantic slave trade from 1519 to 1867, see David Eltis's article "The Volume and Structure of the Transatlantic Slave Trade" (hereafter VS), table III. Teachers who recognize the need to expand their classes beyond the United States to include a wider view of slavery should know the larger study by David Eltis, *The Rise of African Slavery in the Americas*, and John Thornton, *Africa and Africans in the Making of the Atlantic World, 1400–1800*, a book that challenged the old view of Africans helplessly taken in slavery by white raiders, and instead gave a textured view of Africans involved in all aspects of slavery on both sides of the ocean.

*p. 63* For the 1565 wedding feast, see TB, pages 237–38, and, more generally, the essay of which they are a part: Eddy Stols, "The Expansion of the Sugar Market in Western Europe."

*p. 64* For Wickham's letter, see Antony Wild, *The East India Company* (hereafter EIC), page 31. This lavishly illustrated book is a great place for readers from eighth grade up to begin research on tea and its place in world history. For the expansion of tea drinking in England, see page 40; for American tea drinking, see page 144. For the three new hot drinks and their need for sugar, see SP, pages 108–9.

*p. 65* For a chart of the expansion of sugar consumption in England between 1700 and 1809, see SP, page 67.

*p. 67* For "become an economical substitute," see SP, page 114. The paragraphs in which we discuss England, sugar, slavery, and the Industrial Revolution summarize decades of intense discussion and debate among scholars.

An AP or IB teacher could make great use of this historiographical debate, which began with Eric Williams, a famous historian of the Caribbean. In *Capitalism and Slavery*, Williams claimed that, in effect, the Industrial Revolution was a form of theft—that by enslaving Africans, England gained the wealth that allowed it to leap ahead to the next stage of economic development. We consulted his *From Columbus to Castro* (hereafter FCC), which is a readable and informed view of the entire region, though rather dated. Generations of scholars then challenged Williams's argument. More recently, Joseph Inikori has taken full and careful account of the entire range of discussion around the Williams theory and arrived at his own revised version of the connections among sugar, slavery, and the Industrial Revolution. Dr. Inikori shows how the world of commerce across the Atlantic, involving the products of African enslaved labor in the New World, created new markets, new trade relations, new income, which then allowed specific regions of England to focus on manufacturing cloth in factories. He kindly sent us his "Slavery and Atlantic Commerce, 1650–1800," in *American Economic Review*, and directed us to *Africans and the Industrial Revolution in England*, his book-length study. The argument we trace here is the briefest outline of what we learned from his work.

While the positions taken by historians will be of most interest to teachers and students who intend to study history in college, linking the story of sugar and slavery with that of factories and industry makes sense for all high school classes.

*p. 67* Linking tea and sugar with the Industrial Revolution is a key theme of SP; see pages 130–31 for a summary.

*pp. 68–69* For world production of sugar in 1800 and 1900, see SP, page 73. For average consumption in England, see Felicity Lawrence, "Sugar Rush," in *Guardian*; for U.S. consumption, broken down by kind of sweetener, see Stephen Haley et al., "Sweetener Consumption in the United States," USDA study SSS-243-01, available at www.ers.usda.gov.

*p. 71* Pauline was known by her mistress's last name, which we have omitted to avoid confusion. We found her story in D, pages 6–28, and that of Pierre Lemerre the Younger on page 27. The great academic study of the intertwined story of slavery and freedom in this period is David Brion Davis, *The Problem of Slavery in the Age of Revolution, 1770–1823*. This is a central book that any college student will need to know, and that AP and IB teachers can mine for key issues, stories, and ideas. Dr. Davis was challenged by professor Thomas Haskell on the question of the motivations of the abolitionists. Their fascinating conflict of historical interpretation was published in Thomas Bender, ed., *The Antislavery Debate*. The subjects in this book would serve as an ideal focus for discussion in an AP or IB class.

*p. 73* The place of the Sugar Act in the run-up to the American Revolution can be found in Edmund Morgan and Helen Morgan, *The Stamp Act Crisis* (hereafter SAC), pages 21–53. The story of the *Polly* is well told on pages 41–53. Anyone who wants to go a step deeper than the summaries in standard textbooks will find this a rewarding read.

*p. 74* For Beckford, and his wealth, nickname, and influence, see BTC, page 139; see also FCC, pages 132, 135, 223.

*p. 76* For "If Taxes," see SAC, page 35.

*p. 77* The gripping story of the struggle to end the slave trade and then to abolish slavery in England is brilliantly described in BTC. This is a book any high school teacher can and should use—perhaps to accompany M. T. Anderson's stellar Octavian Nothing novels. For "A thought," see BTC, page 89; "In the day-time," page 88. The year 2007 was the bicentennial of the British abolition of the slave trade, and many museums in England created exhibits on slavery, sugar, and abolition. Their websites are rich resources, often including materials for teachers and for students: good historical background, and objects to look at. For example, go to slavetrade.parliament.uk/slavetrade/learning/externallinks/slavery relatedsiteswelike.html and, as linked on that site, www.understandingslavery.com. Readers from middle school up can find much to learn on these sites. AP and IB teachers will also want to use Seymour Drescher, *The Mighty Experiment*, an award-winning academic study that cuts through some of the debates among scholars to give a clear, detailed picture of abolition in England.

*p. 78* For "blood-sweetened," see BTC, page 194. For the boycott, see BTC, pages 192–95; for "FREEMEN," see BTC, page 194.

*pp. 80–81* Back in the late 1980s, Marc had the good fortune to work with Susan Banfield on her young adult book *The Rights of Man, the Reign of Terror* (hereafter ROM). As Susan told the story of the French Revolution, she made sure to keep track of where the various governments of France stood on the question of slavery. The many timelines in that book made it easy for us to outline the issue here. Though the book is long out of print, it is still a fine resource for any middle or high school library. For "Men are born," see page 52.

*p. 83* The history of Haiti is not easily accessible for younger readers. When Marc was growing up, he read heroic—or at least satisfyingly bloody and pulse-pounding—stories about Toussaint and Henri Christophe in, for example, Richard Halliburton's fantasy travel books. But scholars have taken apart many myths about Haiti, leaving a harder-to-follow tangle of evidence and interpretation. While ultimately the enslaved Africans fought for freedom, the issue was, in every sense, far from black and white. The sides included people of color who sometimes owned slaves, local whites who did or did not want more independence from France, the Spanish, French royalists and French revolutionaries, etc. The novelist Madison Smartt Bell wrote an adult biography called *Toussaint Louverture* that does its best to keep all the parties straight but that we found hard going. For our purposes, the engaging writing about the revolt in BTC was once again the best resource. For "and listen" and "a rain of fire," see page 257.

*p. 84* For the song, see Jeannette Marks, *The Family of the Barrett*, page 268; it is also quoted in a different context in SBH, page 84.

*p. 86* For "At our tables," see Richard Sheridan, "The Jamaican Slave Insurrection Scare of 1776 and the American Revolution," in Dubois and Scott, *Origins of the Black Atlantic*, page 36; for the role of black sailors, see Julius Scott, "'Negroes in Foreign Bottoms': Sailors, Slaves and Communication" in the same volume.

To hear samples of music recorded in surviving maroon communities in modern Jamaica, go to the Smithsonian Folkways website and listen to samples from "Drums of Defiance." www.folkways.si.edu/albumdetails.aspx?itemid=2310.

*p. 86* For "prevent a circulation," see BTC, page 268.

*p. 87* For the African background of the fighters, see BTC, page 271.
*p. 87* For "We are fighting," see BTC, page 278.

*p. 89* For "Unless something is done," see Thomas Bender, *A Nation Among Nations*, page 109. Dr. Bender was Marc's doctoral adviser in graduate school and has been an ongoing inspiration for combining U.S. and world history. IB or AP teachers interested in opening up and expanding a U.S. history course so that it links with world history will find many useful leads, ideas, and resources in this book.

A great starting point for research on the connections between the United States and the Haitian Revolution is this brilliant essay written by seventh-grader Jim Thomson. It won the Junior Division of the National History Day prize competition in 2000: "The Haitian Revolution and the Forging of America," in *The History Teacher*.

*p. 91* For "the popular sentiment," see BTC, page 305; for "God can turn," same page; for "sense of the nation," see page 307.

*p. 92* For Ellen Betts, see B. A. Botkin, ed., *Lay My Burden Down*, page 127. This book is a compilation of the recollections of former slaves, which were taken down in the 1930s. It is an invaluable resource for hearing their voices, though historians stress that these are the words of elderly people recounting experiences and events from sixty or more years earlier. An excellent website for the history of sugar in Louisiana, with primary source documents and images, is www.lib.lsu.edu/special/exhibits/sugar/contents.html. It is based on a museum exhibit that was housed at Louisiana State University. Any teacher or student who wants to know more about the history of sugar and slavery in Louisiana should know Richard Follett, *The Sugar Masters* (hereafter SM). Like so many academic books, it contains personal stories and a level of detail that would be otherwise very hard to find. For Ceceil George, see page 46.

*p. 94* For "suckling gang" (Follett's term), see SM, page 98.

*p. 94* For "all de master," see SM, page 67; for "Rachel had," see page 69.

*p. 98* These translations of *holehole bushi* were given to us by Dr. Franklin Odo. They will appear in the forthcoming book *Voices from the Canefields*, which consists of songs collected by Harry Urata and translated by Dr. Odo. It is to come out with an accompanying DVD so that you can hear old-timers sing the songs. The 1995 feature film *Picture Bride* is based on careful research about sugar workers in Hawaii and would make an excellent classroom resource for high school students (some of the events are emotionally wrenching, and some of the songs rather raunchy in a playful way); in addition, the website created to accompany the film, www. picturebridemovie.com, is still active and features essays and historical background that will be useful for students and teachers alike.

The Internet offers several ways to explore Indian indenture. You may start with: www.indocaribbeanheritage.com/component/option .com_zoom/Itemid.76/catid.2/PageNo.3/. This is a BBC documentary about indenture: www.youtube.com/watch?v=FwZNJbTs7BQ& feature=related. And these are other related YouTube videos: www.youtube.com/watch?v=YpxCZRIIJTI&feature=related www.youtube.com/watch?v=8alcewP1Lqk&feature=related www.youtube.com/watch?v=Z3IuPByPXck

*p. 106* For Bharath, see Noor Kumar Mahabir, *The Still Cry*.

*p. 108* The song was copied down by Marina from an exhibition on the Indian diaspora at the Manav Vikas Sangrahalaya (the Museum of the Development of Man), curated in collaboration with the Royal Tropical Institute, Amsterdam, the Netherlands, and housed at the G. B. Pant Institute of Social Sciences, Allahabad, India.

*p. 108* For more information on indenture, see *A New System of Slavery*, by Hugh Tinker.

*p. 112* For the information on Bechu, see *Bechu*, by Clem Seecharan.

*p. 114* The basic outline of the beet sugar story is in every book we have listed—for example, B, pages 131–36. And for the mechanics of processing, see www.sucrose.com/lbeet.html.

*p. 115* (Sugar Genius sidebar) The story of Norbert Rillieux is easy to find on the Internet. We used www.gibbsmagazine.com/Rillieux.htm.

*p. 116* We had hoped to find out enough about beets in Russia to test Marc's family story, and to track down specific names and places. Unfortunately, we did not have the language skills or the access to archives to do so, and we could not find a scholar to help us. For more general information on beets in Russia and Ukraine, we used Questia to dip into resources such as S. G. Pushkarev, *The Emergence of Modern Russia, 1801–1917*, pages 46 and 280; Jesse Clarkson, *A History of Russia*, page 282; and Konstantyn Kononenko, *Ukraine and Russia*, pages 123–26.

*p. 117* For this rapid tour of sugar in the Age of Science, see "Artificial Sweeteners: A History," at hubpages.com/hub/Artificial-Sweeteners-A-History; for the uses of sugar cane in Brazil today, see Alexandra A. Seno, "Business: The Truth About Sugar," in *Newsweek International*, May 1, 2006.

# BIBLIOGRAPHY

Abbott, Elizabeth. *Sugar: A Bittersweet History*. Toronto, Ont.: Penguin Books Canada, 2008. (SBH)

Ambrose, Stephen. *Undaunted Courage*. New York: Simon & Schuster, 1966.

Ashdown, Peter. *Caribbean History in Maps*. Trinidad: Longman Caribbean, 1979.

Banfield, Susan. *The Rights of Man, the Reign of Terror: The Story of the French Revolution*. New York: Lippincott, 1989. (ROM)

Barksdale, Richard, and Keneth Kinnamon, eds. *Black Writers of America*. New York: Macmillan, 1972. Contains *The Interesting Narrative of the Life of Olaudah Equiano, or Gustavus Vassa, the African*. (IN)

Bell, Madison Smartt. *Toussaint Louverture: A Biography*. New York: Pantheon Books, 2007.

Bender, Thomas. *The Antislavery Debate: Capitalism and Abolitionism as a Problem in Historical Interpretation*. Berkeley: University of California Press, 1992.

———, ed. *A Nation Among Nations: America's Place in World History*. New York: Hill and Wang, 2006.

Boissonnade, P. *Life and Work in Medieval Europe (Fifth to Fifteenth Centuries)*. Translated by Eileen Power. London: Kegan Paul, Trench, 1927.

Botkin, B. A., ed. *Lay My Burden Down: A Folk History of Slavery*. Chicago: University of Chicago Press, 1945.

Burnard, Trevor G. *Mastery, Tyranny, and Desire: Thomas Thistlewood and His Slaves in the Anglo-Jamaican World*. Chapel Hill: University of North Carolina Press, 2004. (MTD)

Burney, David, and Lida Pigott Burney. "Charcoal Stratigraphies for Kuai'i and the Timing of Human Arrival." *Pacific Studies* 57, no. 2: 211–26.

Burrows, Edwin, and Mike Wallace. *Gotham: A History of New York City to 1898*. New York: Oxford University Press, 2000.

Clarkson, Jesse Dunsmore. *A History of Russia*. New York: Random House, 1961.

Curtin, Philip D. *The Rise and Fall of the Plantation Complex*. 2nd ed. Cambridge: Cambridge University Press, 1998. (RFP)

Davis, David Brion. *The Problem of Slavery in the Age of Revolution, 1770–1823.* Ithaca, N.Y.: Cornell University Press, 1975.

Drescher, Seymour. *The Mighty Experiment: Free Labor vs. Slavery in British Emancipation.* New York: Oxford University Press, 2002.

Dubois, Laurent, and Julius S. Scott, eds. *Origins of the Black Atlantic.* New York: Routledge, 2010.

Eltis, David. *The Rise of African Slavery in the Americas.* Cambridge: Cambridge University Press, 2000.

———. "The Volume and Structure of the Transatlantic Slave Trade: A Reassessment." *William and Mary Quarterly* 58, no. 1 ( January 2001): 17–46. (VS)

Favier, Jean. *Gold and Spices: The Rise of Commerce in the Middle Ages.* Translated by Caroline Higgitt. New York: Holmes & Meier, 1998.

Feltoe, Richard. *Redpath: The History of a Sugar House.* Toronto, Ont.: Dundum Press, 1991.

Follett, Richard. *The Sugar Masters: Planters and Slaves in Louisiana's Cane World, 1820–1860.* Baton Rouge: Louisiana State University Press, 2005. (SM)

Freedman, Paul. *Out of the East: Spices and the Medieval Imagination.* New Haven, Conn.: Yale University Press, 2008. (OE)

Funari, Pedro Paulo, Martin Hall, and Siân Jones, eds. *Historical Archaeology: Back from the Edge.* New York: Routledge, 1999.

Hall, Douglas. *In Miserable Slavery: Thomas Thistlewood in Jamaica, 1750–86.* Barbados: University of the West Indies Press, 1999.

Harms, Robert. *The Diligent: A Voyage Through the Worlds of the Slave Trade.* New York: Basic Books, 2002. (D)

Hochschild, Adam. *Bury the Chains: Prophets and Rebels in the Fight to Free an Empire's Slaves.* Boston: Houghton Mifflin, 2005. (BTC)

Humphrey, John W., John P. Oleson, and Andrew N. Sherwood. *Greek and Roman Technology: A Sourcebook: Annotated Translations of Greek and Latin Texts and Documents.* London: Routledge, 1998.

Inikori, Joseph E. *Africans and the Industrial Revolution in England: A Study in International Trade and Economic Development.* Cambridge: Cambridge University Press, 2002.

———. "Slavery and Atlantic Commerce, 1650–1800." *American Economic Review* 82, no. 2, 151–57.

Klein, Herbert S. *African Slavery in Latin America and the Caribbean.* New York: Oxford University Press, 1988.

Kononenko, Konstantyn. *Ukraine and Russia: A History of the Economic Relations Between Ukraine and Russia, 1654–1917.* Milwaukee, Wisc.: Marquette University Press, 1958.

Lawrence, Felicity. "Sugar Rush." *Guardian,* February 15, 2007.

Macinnis, Peter. *Bittersweet: The Story of Sugar.* Crows Nest, Australia: Allen & Unwin, 2002. (B)

Magoun, H. W. "The Asuri-Kalpa: A Witchcraft Practice of the Atharva-Veda." *American Journal of Philology* 10, no. 2 (1889), 165–97.

Mahabir, Noor Kumar, *The Still Cry: Personal Accounts of East Indians in Trinidad and Tobago During Indentureship, 1845–1917.* Tacarigua, Trinidad: Calaloux Publications, 1985.

Marks, Jeannette. *The Family of the Barrett: A Colonial Romance.* New York: Macmillan, 1938.

Menninger, Karl. *Number Words and Number Symbols: A Cultural History of Numbers.* Translated by Paul Broneer. Cambridge, Mass.: MIT Press, 1969. Reprint, New York: Dover Press, 1992.

Mintz, Sidney W. *Sweetness and Power: The Place of Sugar in Modern History.* New York: Viking, 1985. (SP)

Morgan, Edmund, and Helen M. Morgan. *The Stamp Act Crisis: Prologue to Revolution.* Chapel Hill: University of North Carolina Press, 1953. 2nd ed. with new introduction, 1995. (SAC)

Pirenne, Henri. *Economic and Social History of Medieval Europe.* New York: Harcourt Brace, 1954.

Polo, Marco. *The Travels of Marco Polo.* Translated by Ronald Latham. London: Penguin, 1958.

Pushkarev, S. G. *The Emergence of Modern Russia, 1801–1917.* Translated by Robert H. McNeal and Tova Yedin. New York: Holt Rinehart and Winston, 1963.

Schwartz, Stuart B., ed. *Slaves, Peasants, and Rebels: Reconsidering Brazilian Slavery.* Urbana: University of Illinois Press, 1996.

———, ed. *Tropical Babylons: Sugar and the Making of the Atlantic World, 1450–1680.* Chapel Hill: University of North Carolina Press, 2004. (TB)

Seecharan, Clem. *Bechu: "Bound Coolie" Radical in British Guiana 1894–1901,*

The University of the West Indies Press, Kingston, Jamaica, 1999.

Sheridan, Richard B. "Africa and the Caribbean in the Atlantic Slave Trade." *American Historical Review* 77, no. 1 (February 1972): 15–35. (ACAS)

———. *Sugar and Slavery: An Economic History of the British West Indies, 1623–1775.* Kingston, Jamaica: University of the West Indies Press, 1994. (SS)

Stols, Eddy. "The Expansion of the Sugar Market in Western Europe."

Strong, L.A.G. *The Story of Sugar.* London: Weidenfeld and Nicholson, 1954.

Thomson, Jim. "The Haitian Revolution and the Forging of America." *History Teacher* 34, no. 1 (Nov. 2000): www.historycooperative.org/journals/ht/34.1/thomson.html.

Tinker, Hugh. *A New System of Slavery: The Export of Indian Labour Overseas, 1830–1920.* London: Oxford University Press, 1974.

Thornton, John. *Africa and Africans in the Making of the Atlantic World, 1400–1800.* New York: Cambridge University Press, 1992. 2nd ed., 1998.

Urata, Harry. *Voices from the Canefields: Folksongs from Japanese Immigrant Workers in Hawai'i.* Translated by Dr. Franklin Odo, forthcoming.

Wild, Antony. *The East India Company: Trade and Conquest from 1600.* New York: Lyons Press, 2000. (EIC)

———. *From Columbus to Castro: The History of the Caribbean, 1492–1969.* New York: Random House, 1970. Reprint, New York: Vintage Press, 1984. (FCC)

# Websites

Here are some articles on websites that we consulted as background research:

"How Sugar Is Made—the History" (note that this and the next two are all pages within the same site): www.sucrose.com/lhist.html (brief summary of sugar history with a few illustrations)

"How Sugar Is Made": www.sucrose.com/ltypes.html (about various types of sugar)

"How Sugar Is Made—an Introduction": www.sucrose.com/learn.html (includes an interactive map showing where sugar is made today)

"Sugar," by J. H. Galloway; entry in *The Cambridge World History of Food*, edited by Kenneth F. Kiple and Kriemhild Coneè Ornelas: www.cambridge.org/us/ books/kiple/sugar.htm (a good adult-oriented encyclopedia entry, useful for background research)

"Sugar Cane—History": www.plantcultures.org.uk/plants/ sugar_cane_history.html (though the article is quite short, we found ourselves returning to this site to read about sugar in Asia)

"The High Price of Sugar," by Susan Miller; *Newsweek* Special Issue, Fall/Winter 1991, pp. 70–74: www.muweb.millersville.edu/~columbus/data/art/ MILLER01.ART (a good summary of the high human price of slave-made sugar)

"Norbert Rillieux," by Susan Robinson: www.gibbsmagazine.com/Rillieux.htm

# INDEX

*Note:* Page numbers in **bold** type refer to illustrations.